POWERTALK!

HOW TO SPEAK IT, THINK IT, AND USE IT

by Jeffrey Eisen, Ph.D.

with Pat Farley

A FIRESIDE BOOK

PUBLISHED BY SIMON & SCHUSTER, INC.
NEW YORK

Copyright © 1984 by Jeffrey Eisen
All rights reserved
including the right of reproduction
in whole or in part in any form
First Fireside Edition, 1986
Published by Simon & Schuster, Inc.
Simon & Schuster Building
Rockefeller Center
1230 Avenue of the Americas
New York, New York 10020

FIRESIDE and colophon
are registered trademarks of Simon & Schuster, Inc.

Manufactured in the United States of America

10 9 8 7 6 5 4 3 2

Library of Congress Cataloging-in-Publication Data

Eisen, Jeffrey.
  Powertalk! : how to speak it, think it, and use it.

  Reprint. Originally published: New York :
Cornerstone Library, © 1984.
  "A Fireside book."
  Includes index.
  1. Oral communication.   2. Interpersonal
communication.   3. Control (Psychology)   I. Farley, Pat.
II. Title.   III. Title: Power talk!
P95.E37   1986   001.54′2   86-14274
ISBN: 0-671-63276-0

To Lew Sherwood

CONTENTS

Preface *ix*

1 Conversation and the Power Dimension *1*

2 Test Your Power Quotient *13*

3 Emphatics: The Way Powertalkers Say
What They Think *21*

4 Power Words from Power Worlds *40*

5 The Powertalk Delivery *54*

6 The Powertalk Style *70*

7 Powertalkers Use the Sound of Reason *84*

8 Taking Power *96*

9 Rebalancing the Power in Your Life *105*

10 Powertalk and the Outside World *116*

11 Powertalk Between Family, Friends, and Lovers *128*

12 Powertalk in Business *151*

13 Powertalking Your Way into a
Raise and Promotion *163*

14 Powertalk Salesmanship *185*

15 From Powertalk to Personal Power *200*

Speak Powertalk
for Real Assertiveness!

Of all the problems people have in their face-to-face interactions, lack of assertiveness is probably the most prevalent, and one of the most important.

Employees need it to get fair treatment from their bosses; wives need it to set limits on their husbands, and vice versa; children need it to protect themselves from bullying peers; and we all need it to avoid being taken advantage of by parents, friends, our children, doctors, lawyers, and just about every other person with whom we come into contact.

Assertiveness is necessary to protect ourselves and set limits on others, but it has another more important use. It is the means by which we impose our will on other people. It is the way we get them to respect us, to listen to what we have to say, and to do what we need them to do.

All of us, whether in our work or our personal lives, are called upon to relate assertively on a daily basis, in order to accomplish one task or another. And all of us could greatly benefit from learning how to communicate assertiveness more effectively.

Ever since psychologists and other experts in human relations have begun to help people deal with one another better, they have been talking and writing about assertiveness in one form or another. In recent years, however, assertiveness training has become widespread. Dozens of books have been written with titles like *Winning Through Intimidation*, and *Don't Say Yes When You Want to Say No*, and every neighborhood YMCA offers assertiveness workshops.

These books and training programs have concentrated on various aspects of the assertiveness process—from how to feel assertive and master the body language of assertion to strategies you can use when other people are trying to be assertive with you.

In the course of my work as a psychotherapist and career counselor, I have worked with many people who have read these books and taken the workshops. I discovered that any improvement in their assertiveness was extremely uneven at best. They professed a much more assertive philosophy of human relations and thought about their lives in a more assertive manner, but when it came time to actually communicate assertively, they couldn't do it.

The pattern was fairly consistent. Time after time they would begin an interaction, psyched for action and ready to fight to the death if necessary, and then halfway through it they would begin to falter. Somehow they would lose belief in their positions and be pulled around to the positions of their opponents.

As I worked with these people, both privately and in workshops using role playing and simulation techniques, I discovered something very interesting. The crux of the problem was not in their intentions or attitudes, but in their language. In some ways their language was defeating them. It seemed to be simultaneously undermining their own resolve and betraying their weaknesses to their opponents.

I then started taping sessions and analyzing them. What I and my coworkers heard was really quite astonishing. It was almost as if people had two different personalities. One of these personalities spoke in a way which sounded assertive, and the other spoke in a way which sounded submissive. People seemed to alternate from one of these ways of speaking to the other, and the transitions seemed to have something to do with how mentally strong they were feeling at the moment.

In addition, there were periods when the two ways of speaking would seem to get jumbled together. This seemed to happen at transition points. To make things even more complicated, people seldom spoke exclusively in an assertive fashion. They frequently mixed submissive speech into it, and these submissive intrusions seemed to provide openings for their opponents.

These interesting discoveries stimulated me to start both experimenting and brushing up my psycholinguistics to further my investigation. Before long I was deeply involved in developing the theories and practices that revolutionized the way I taught people assertiveness, which I will convey to you here.

The core of my research indicated two points:

First. The English language is indeed spoken in two modes. One of these modes is used when we are relating to others dominantly—the assertive mode. The other is used when we are relating to others submissively—the submissive mode. I call these modes *powertalk* and *subtalk*.

Second. Relating assertively is inseparable from speaking assertively. YOU CANNOT REALLY SUCCEED AT BEING ASSERTIVE UNLESS YOU MASTER POWERTALK!

Powertalk and subtalk are both standard English, but they are spoken in distinctive and different ways. People construct their sentences differently, choose different vocabulary, and speak with a different cadence and intonation when they are speaking powertalk as opposed to speaking subtalk.

Whenever we speak subtalk, or whenever we let elements of subtalk creep into our attempts to speak powertalk, other people hear us as being submissive no matter how hard we try to sound assertive. Their tendency will be to try to ignore what we say and do, and try to dominate us in turn. This obviously defeats our attempts to relate assertively.

On the other hand, when we speak powertalk people perceive us as being dominant and strong. They feel respectful and, to the degree that they are of a submissive nature, have the impulse to submit to us.

In order to really function assertively, we must learn all about powertalk and subtalk—their syntax, vocabulary, organization, and usage. We must become aware of when and why we speak subtalk, and purge it from our speech. And we must develop skill in using powertalk when we are confronting someone who is trying to dominate us.

The utilization of powertalk will make a major shift in the way we communicate and in the way we are perceived. We will become much more effective in all our interactions, and people will respond to us much more positively.

This will help to fulfill our wants and needs in every interaction in our lives, whether they are with employer or employees, professionals or clients, husband or wife, children or parents, friends or adversaries.

POWERTALK!

CONVERSATION AND THE POWER DIMENSION

█

I know I'm at least as smart as the rest of my friends, but I can't seem to get anyone to take my opinions seriously.

We never seem to do anything I want.

Even though I'm the boss, everyone ignores my orders and does everything their own way. It drives me crazy.

All of my children give me backtalk.

I've been with the company a long time, and I know I'm valued there, but somehow the really good promotions seem to pass me by.

Almost all of us find ourselves making the above statements from time to time. Are your desires, requests, and even demands often disregarded without reason, and your ideas and opinions overlooked? Do you frequently find yourself following the leadership of others, when you feel the leadership position should rightfully be yours? Wouldn't life be easier, to say nothing of more fun, if others gave you more respect without your having to fight for it? How would you like to be able to dominate people and situations whenever you feel the need to, and share the power equally the rest of the time? Don't you deserve to be treated as an equal by other effective and successful people? "Sounds good," you may find yourself thinking. However, you may ask: "Once personality patterns like mine are set, aren't they set for life? Isn't it almost impossible to change the way people respond to me?"

The answer, surprisingly, is no. In most cases, the reason no one listens to you, does what you ask, lets you finish a sentence, or grants you codominant equality is due simply to the way you are speaking the language. The way in which you express yourself tells others if they can get away with ignoring you, or treating you like a powerless person. By speaking the language of submission, you are telling others that you don't believe you're entitled to anything. And the world, thus informed, will treat you accordingly.

However, if you speak the language of power, you'll get the respect and courtesy which you desire. You'll be treated as a powerful equal, entitled to be heard, with worthwhile ideas. When you want, you'll be able to dominate conversations and even relationships, take control, be a leader.

To a great extent, power is just a matter of how you express yourself. And the purpose of this book is to teach you this language of power—a special dialect of the English language that I call *powertalk*—and to show you how to use powertalk strategically to get what you want out of life.

Powertalk is composed of the way you construct your sentences, the words you use, how your voice sounds, body language, and how you put it all together in dealing with another person. It sounds complicated but, in fact, it's a dialect you already know! Every day, in every encounter with another person, we either hear or speak powertalk. It's a major part of the hidden language that scientists have only recently begun to investigate. Because no one has ever analyzed how to speak and use it, however, it's always been an instinctive part of the total behavioral and conversational pattern.

You can always recognize powertalk when you hear it. Based upon what you hear, you automatically understand how much power the other person is accustomed to having and whether you are viewed as an equal, a superior, or a subordinate.

Once you consciously understand powertalk, however, you'll be able to use it deliberately and establish the kind of relationships *you* want.

Power Is the Key to Dominance _____

Powertalk makes you sound like you have power, whether you actually do or not. Others believe that a person with power is:

1. A person of value—with special skills, knowledge, authority, or some useful quality that's desirable. A power person is, in short, someone people want to know and be associated with.

2. A person to be reckoned with—someone who walks tall and can't be lightly dismissed. A power person is perceived as someone with the will and the authority to demand a hearing and fair treatment, whatever the situation.

A person with power is someone who has what is known as a dominant personality, and tends towards the leadership role whenever there's an opportunity. Dominants may function as codominants with other dominant people. In personal relationships, particularly, the ideal is a partnership of forceful, powerful, positive codominants where each party has the respect, equality, and consideration to which he or she is entitled.

In contrast, people without power have submissive personalities. Their natural tendency is to appease, placate, and submit to others. They're uncertain of the value of their opinions, ideas, skills, and knowledge—or worse yet, they devalue these power bases and consider them insignificant or lacking qualities such as perfection. As a result, they present themselves fearfully or hesitantly, often seeking approval and respect through modesty, pleasing others, and performing a supporting role. (They communicate all this by using a dialect I call *subtalk,* the language of submission.)

The result of being nice, respectful, and hopeful that others will recognize your value is that no one does, nor will they respect you. They won't let you direct, lead, instruct, or negotiate. They won't even let you be an equal partner unless they are also a submissive type (and such a relationship is weakening to both).

Obviously, it's preferable to be a dominant person. When I studied to become a psychotherapist, I was taught that people were dominant or submissive types. This meant you were forever either a person with power who could live life your way or a person without power, doing what others told you to do. As the years went by and I practiced my profession, however, I realized this wasn't true at all. Although some people are habitually much more dominant than others, no one is inherently dominant or submissive. Actually, most people switch from one role to the other regularly—they're dominant in some parts of their lives, submissive in others. Children, for instance, are often submissive with their parents and teachers yet very dominant with their playmates. The mailroom clerk may be the most submissive person in the office but ruler of the castle at home and a leader at a local club.

Once I realized that everyone has the potential for dominance and submissiveness, I wondered why people couldn't take power and be dominant whenever they wanted. What was the clerk doing at home that made him (or her) a respected local club president who was carefully listened to by all members? And what did the clerk do differently in the office that caused people to pass him over for promotion time and time again, ignore what he had to say and dismiss him as someone of no account?

The Decision to Take Power

At first I thought dominance and submissiveness were determined by a complex combination of many different factors such as upbringing, sex, size, ability, looks, socioeconomic status, education, profession, and background. But while all these things were part of it, they didn't really explain how people decided who was the leader and who was the follower so quickly. Then I came across a discovery so major, so powerful, that it completely changed how I viewed power: YOU MAKE THE DECISION! And what's more, the moment you decide you're going to be dominant or submissive, you communicate your decision to everyone else!

It's very much like what happens among other social animals (who all use a system of signaling to communicate with one another—a very simple form of powertalk). When one dog meets another, they *always* determine who's going to be the dominant dog. As soon as the decision is made, they communicate it. The submissive one looks away, not meeting the other's eyes. It may even roll over on its back to expose throat and belly. It hunches over to make itself small and nonthreatening. The dominant dog stares aggressively, may bare its teeth and make itself larger by standing stiff-legged and raising its hackles. Each animal chooses its role, and often it's the submissive dog who makes the first move, gesturing defeat and handing over power before the other dog does anything. When both dogs choose the dominant role, they engage in a power struggle. They make threatening gestures toward one another, finally culminating in a fight that escalates in ferocity. If one dog submits and acknowledges the leadership of the other, the struggle immediately ceases.

Being human beings, our system is a bit more complex and subtle, offering solutions other than the boss/slave relationship of dogs. Yet we still establish power relationships with every person we meet, in every encounter. We always have a choice either to submit and be treated as a subordinate, or to demand acceptance as a power person and take a dominant or codominant role. Even if you've never been in a position of power in your life, you can choose to be dominant with the next person you meet. You can put down this book, walk into the kitchen, and change power positions with your spouse right now (although changing an existing power structure can be tricky and it would be better to read on to find out how to do this pleasantly).

Powertalk and Subtalk Are How You Signal Your Choice

Instead of using the gestures of dogs, humans employ language dialects to signal their decisions on whether to submit or dominate. Your decision is in your tone of voice, the way in which you pose a question or answer one, how you present topics for decision, the way you phrase your sentences, your choice of words, your tendency to pause, interrupt, or be interrupted, your body language, and how you handle each stage of a conversation. If you intend to be dominant, you speak powertalk; if you intend to submit you use subtalk.

Powertalk and subtalk have little to do with the substance of what you're saying. That part of a conversation is almost a smoke screen for this hidden dimension. You could be presenting yourself as interested, fair, and equalitarian while you're actually asserting control. You might be making idle chitchat about the weather, apparently marking time, while making a bid for dominance. Or your explicit message may even be just the opposite of what you're actually communicating. For example, you might say, "Look, I'm the boss and I say you do it this way," while your hidden message is that you don't feel comfortable being boss, you're not used to power, and you're perfectly willing to back down if a little pressure is applied.

To show how powertalk and subtalk work, the following is an expansion of this example in both dialects:

A POWERTALKER IS THE BOSS

BOSS: *Do it this way!*
SUBORDINATE: *But . . .*
BOSS (interrupting): *No but's. We'll do it this way and that's that. Now I've got another meeting to get to so let's finish up.*

A SUBTALKER IS THE BOSS

BOSS: *Well, look, I really think . . . I mean it really would be better, in my opinion, and I do have a lot of experience in this, if we did it this way.*
SUBORDINATE: *I just don't think it's going to work that way.*
BOSS: *Oh, it seems to me it will. It has before, after all, hasn't it? And, well, I am in charge and I do think you ought to . . . you know . . . let's do it this way, don't you think?*
SUBORDINATE: *But you put me in charge of it and that should give me the right to do it the way I think best.*

Notice that by hemming and hawing, equivocating and otherwise weakening all statements, the subtalking boss invites the subordinate to argue and try to take control. That's how these dialects work!

Even though you haven't been aware that you were doing it until now, you're very skilled at communicating on this hidden level. The trouble is that because power-talk and subtalk are usually spoken unconsciously, people tend to automatically fall into roles. Many people have come to think of themselves so exclusively in the submissive role that they rarely use powertalk; when they do use it, they speak so haltingly and without conviction that others don't respond to it with normal reactions. Good powertalkers just steamroll right over them, forcing them back to subtalk and submission. This is why people who should have power, respect, and honor by rights of hard-won achievement, knowledge, position, or wealth often don't have real power and can't effectively command or count others as true codominant equals.

Such people—and they're the majority of us—are substantially impaired, if not completely blocked in their attempts to rise to positions of power in their work. Even with friends and family they may have a submissive role rather than an equalitarian relationship. If these people do rise to positions which require command, they're usually awkward, uncomfortable, not very effective, and they frequently fail.

Powertalk Can Transform Your Life _____

If you're like most people, you will discover that your Power Quotient, your ability to speak powertalk, can be improved. Powertalk can make a very real difference in your life. We all recognize those who speak powertalk naturally and well. We think of them as born leaders, people who will go far in life. These natural powertalkers seem to be born to power and blessed by fortune. They're often accepted in roles and positions of authority for which they have neither credentials, preparation, nor talent. They may become leaders of industry and society for no other reason than they are able to act aggressively, make decisions, and sound convincing in the part.

Powertalk helps to create such advantages. And the powertalk you learn in this book can turn you, too, into a "born leader." Perhaps it will take you further than the instinctive powertalker because you will have the potential to use powertalk deliberately. You need not rely on instincts and habits. You'll learn exactly what sort of powertalk is called for in any given situation; you'll learn how to combine powertalk with subtalk to motivate people or communicate your leadership abilities. I'll even help you plan your powertalk strategies in advance. And since you're always better at something when you understand what makes it work and how it's used, you can become a powertalk master.

During the process of developing the powertalk concept, I've taught many of my clients powertalk fundamentals. And the results have been surprisingly rapid and extensive. I've seen changes begin even before people use powertalk skillfully. Just recognizing when powertalk and subtalk are being used gives you great insight into your relationships with people. You'll quickly see how much power you actually have in your relationships with spouses, children, relatives and friends, business associates, colleagues and clients, secretaries and bosses. You'll recognize those who take you for granted and don't really respect you or see you as a person with power. You'll see where you're creating problems for yourself, making your own life less pleasant and more difficult.

Understanding and using powertalk need not turn you into a bossy bully who tries to become a petty dictator. Instead, it helps you readjust the power balances in your life and makes life run more smoothly. You'll find your life becomes easier in many small ways when you begin speaking powertalk deliberately, and you'll be able to make major changes by planning power adjustments strategically.

Subtalkers really have a difficult time in life. In the horse world, a herd of horses will be unmerciful to the horse that doesn't stick up for itself. Extremely submissive horses are regularly attacked by all the other horses in the herd; they're driven away from food and may even die from such treatment if humans don't intervene. We don't physically harm our fellow subtalkers, but we take full advantage of them, using their submissiveness to pass off unpleasant tasks, to get our own way, and even to vent hositility and anger that we dare not let loose on more powerful people.

Here are just a few of the changes that you may experience when you start powertalking:

- You'll discover that conversation is more enjoyable when others pay attention to you, when you have the opportunity to talk about what you want, when interruptions are greatly reduced (and you'll learn how to stop them as well), when people care about your opinions and views.

- You'll clarify the nature of your relationships with those close to you. You need not always be a listener, someone who does all the work, the one who always supports and is never supported. With powertalk, you can achieve equality, even dominate if you wish.

- Promotions may come your way faster. Employers are always on the lookout for those with leadership abilities. And, you need not wait to be recognized— powertalk can help you devise strategies to let your boss know you were born to command!

- Getting work done will become far easier when you use powertalk to issue orders to your subordinates. You'll be able to motivate your employees and keep them longer. You'll eliminate backtalk and unnecessary arguments. Your office or department will become a much more pleasant place in which to work.

And use of powertalk in issuing instructions results in fewer errors, misunderstandings, and mix-ups.

● You may suddenly find yourself in demand to chair committees, lead groups, and speak publicly. Power-talkers are instinctively recognized as leaders and people with something important to say. Others will look to you for instruction.

● For anyone in sales, powertalk is a basic necessity for survival. Powertalkers regularly surpass quotas, bring in more new business than anyone else, and increase the sizes of average orders. You'll learn how to use specific powertalk strategies to "command" your prospects to buy!

● You'll understand other people better. You'll learn to read others and see how they use the power dimension. You'll see when people are bluffing and pretending to be what they aren't. You'll learn how to look beyond the substance of a conversation to the hidden powertalk and see when people are using mixed signals to deny what they're trying to do.

● You'll soon count more powerful people as your friends and allies. Power is drawn to power. When you begin speaking powertalk, you'll find that people who used to patronize you, or perhaps not even recognize your existence, now want to count you as an associate. You'll also find that powerful people are more willing to help you, advise you, and support your efforts.

● You'll find it easier to get what you want with fewer annoyances and delays. Powertalk can help you avoid the intimidation of store clerks, government bureaucrats, and other normally supercilious time-wasters. From straightening out aggravating errors on credit and bank statements to dealing with the traffic cop, the plumber, and the tax official, powertalk can smooth your way, speed service, and gain cooperation in settling things *your* way.

And when you speak powertalk, you'll feel more powerful as well. Just think of what happens when you act aggressively, tensing your muscles, thrusting your chin forward, clenching your fists. A psychological switch is thrown and you go into a fight reaction. Adrenalin courses through your system and you feel extremely pugnacious, willing and able to act assertively. Speaking powertalk produces the same effect. You don't just talk like a leader. You feel like one. You are one!

Summary

Powertalk and subtalk are separate dialects of the English language which we all speak and understand on an instinctive level. This book will teach you these dialects and help you to use them deliberately whenever you wish.

Powertalk is the language of power and dominance. It communicates that you are a powerful person who is willing and able to stand up for your opinions, insist on your rights, and demand respect.

Subtalk is the language of submission, telling others that you don't believe in your own self-worth and that you defer to the power of the person to whom you're speaking.

People aren't restricted to being a dominant or submissive type. You are undoubtedly dominant in some areas of your life now and submissive in other ways. With this book, you can use that ability to establish the relationship you want, either as a superior or, more frequently, as a codominant in which you and the other person mutually acknowledge each other's rights and power.

TEST
YOUR POWER QUOTIENT
2

Do You Have the Subtalk Habit? _____

Are you one of the many who speaks subtalk most of the time, unconsciously choosing to surrender power and submit to others in most of your encounters? The measure of your use of powertalk (or subtalk) is your powertalk quotient or PQ. Knowing your PQ will give you an accurate idea of just how much powertalk to use—and tell you how effective you are in conversation. Your PQ will also help you to see how others perceive you, providing a realistic picture of how far you have to go in order to make the changes you want in your life.

The
PQ Test

In order to determine your PQ, answer the following questions. Each question is followed by a scale of one through five since the answers are usually not a definite "yes" or "no" but rather a matter of degree. Circle the number which you feel best represents you. For now, choose the best answer for the way in which you act or feel most of the time. After you finish reading this book, you may wish to retake this test to analyze specific areas of your life, such as your business or family relationships.

This quiz will tell you where to stand on the continuum from being a heavy powertalker to a habitual subtalker. It is for your own information only; there are no right or wrong answers. In the interests of accuracy, the questions have been made very direct. This makes them easy to understand. If you cheat, you will only be defeating the purpose of the test and depriving yourself of valuable information. Resist that temptation.

1. When you want someone to do something for you, do you ask for it directly, or do you ask indirectly by hinting around and hoping they'll understand and do it?

   Indirectly   1   2   3   4   5   Directly

2. When you express an opinion, do you usually hedge it in some way in case you turn out to be wrong, or do you state it flatly?

   Hedge   1   2   3   4   5   Flat out

3. When you want to say something in a conversation, do you usually express it naturally and easily, or do you find yourself either fighting to say it or waiting until everyone else is through talking?

   Fight or wait   1   2   3   4   5   Easily

4. Do you have a lot of verbal mannerisms in your speech, such as "you know," "sort of," "do you think," or "maybe"?

Many   1   2   3   4   5   Few

5. Do you frequently have the feeling that other people don't listen to what you say?

Often   1   2   3   4   5   Seldom

6. Do you usually find yourself going along with other people's suggestions, or do they tend to follow yours?

Go along   1   2   3   4   5   Follow me

7. Do you worry about what to talk about in conversations, or do you feel confident to talk about whatever comes to mind?

Worry   1   2   3   4   5   Confident

8. Do you communicate almost completely with words, or do you spontaneously use gestures and facial expressions?

Words   1   2   3   4   5   Gestures and expressions

9. Do you frequently feel that the conversations you're involved in are unfair because you listen to others, but they don't want to listen to you?

Unfair   1   2   3   4   5   Fair

10. Do you pride yourself in being a good listener?

Yes   1   2   3   4   5   Not particularly

11. Do you often have to ask several times for people to do something for you?

Frequently   1   2   3   4   5   Rarely

12. Do you feel as though people interrupt you more than they do others, and even change the topic of conversation with you?

Often   1   2   3   4   5   Seldom

13. Do people frequently ask you to do favors for them, run errands, or do things that take up a fair amount of time and involve considerable effort?

Often   1   2   3   4   5   Seldom

14. Do people frequently let you down by not living up to your expectations for the right way to act?

Frequently   1   2   3   4   5   Rarely

15. Do people who you are not on intimate terms with often seem to feel they have the right to touch you?

Frequently   1   2   3   4   5   Rarely

16. When you bring up a new topic of conversation, do others usually pick it up?

Seldom   1   2   3   4   5   Usually

17. Do people give you unrequested advice on how to conduct your personal affairs?

Often   1   2   3   4   5   Seldom

18. Are you often in situations where you address someone formally, and they address you by your first name, a nickname, or some diminuative term?

Often   1   2   3   4   5   Seldom

19. Do you try to express your opinions in ways that other people will not find fault with?

Usually 1 2 3 4 5 Seldom

20. When others disagree with you, do you try to find a compromise between your opinions, or do you try to argue them over to your viewpoint?

Compromise 1 2 3 4 5 Argue

21. When you are in a position of authority, do you use expressions such as "I want" and "I think," or do you say things like "It would be best to . . . and "Probably a good idea would be . . . ?"

Probably it would be . . . 1 2 3 4 5 I want

22. Do you frequently make absolute statements like "Always do it like this" or "Never do so and so?"

Seldom 1 2 3 4 5 Frequently

23. "That's a beautiful painting, isn't it?" is a tag question. How often do you think you use tag questions when expressing your opinions?

Often 1 2 3 4 5 Seldom

24. When you state an opinion, do you often soften it by saying, "It's kind of nice," "I'm pretty sure," or "I'm almost positive"?

Usually 1 2 3 4 5 Seldom

25. Do you use a lot of verbal fillers, such as "er," "um," or "you know" when you speak?

Often 1 2 3 4 5 Seldom

26. Do you often begin a statement of opinion with a statement such as "This might sound stupid, but . . ."

or "I know you won't see it this way, but still . . ."?

Often   1   2   3   4   5   Seldom

27. In describing a valued colleague which expression would be more your style?
(a) He's a sensitive and supportive ally.
(b) He is a good team player.

(a)   1   2   3   4   5   (b)

28. If you had promised someone payment by the end of the month, which of the following two expressions would you be more likely to use (assuming you would use one or the other)?
(a) I'll pay you out of my next paycheck.
(b) I've already allocated funds to take care of that.

(a)   1   2   3   4   5   (b)

29. If someone did something against you, and you threatened to get even, would you be more likely to "teach him a lesson" or "kick the crap out of him"?

Teach   1   2   3   4   5   Kick

30. Would you be more likely to describe a given color as purple or mauve?

Mauve   1   2   3   4   5   Purple

31. If something were broken, would you be more likely to talk about the need to mend the break, or repair the break?

Mend   1   2   3   4   5   Repair

Score Yourself

Total the circled numbers to obtain your score. Use the following table to evaluate it.

UNDER 70

You generally speak subtalk. You are overly concerned with people's opinions about you, and generally play a submissive role in your personal relationships. Your style of expression and choice of vocabulary tell other people they can dominate you easily, and they do. You need to effect a dramatic reversal in your verbal strategies in order to be taken as seriously as you want to be, and to earn the success you deserve.

70 TO 100

You are a moderate person—agreeable, but not subservient. You speak a mixture of powertalk and subtalk, but you tend to speak too much subtalk for most purposes. While the mix you speak probably works well for friendships, it leads you to be somewhat taken advantage of in other situations, such as work or dealing with professionals, repairmen, government officials, etc. You need to sharpen up your powertalk considerably, but you should do it selectively, identifying those situations in which you tend to be submissive (one clue is to look for things you are habitually angry about) and working on them first.

100 TO 125

You are a strong, assertive person, and a real powertalker. You tend to dominate in most situations and relationships, or at least to be codominant, and avoid submissiveness. At the same time, you are aware of the other person, and try to hear what they are saying, taking them into account. Your task is to refine your powertalk skills to become even more effective. Look for areas where you might still be submissive, and also be on the lookout for areas where you might overdo it and become tyrannical. With work you could develop into a real leader.

ABOVE 125

This is too much of a good thing. You are used to having other people do your bidding. If anything, your powertalk is stronger than it needs to be. You tend to be bossy, and fail to take into account the feelings and needs of others. You are probably very successful in situations of clear authority, but get into trouble with friends and family, pushing people away, and creating a lot of resentment. You need to analyze your style carefully. Do not become less assertive, but assert yourself in a very considerate and courteous way, and take the time to hear what others have to say. Do not insist on your way unless it is important to you, and you are confident that your demands are fair and justified. Be careful to give those beneath you some freedom to find their own solutions and make their own mistakes. This is important if you are a manager—and even more important if you are a parent.

EMPHATICS:
THE WAY POWERTALKERS
SAY WHAT THEY THINK

3

Directness
and Emphasis Are Basic to All
Powertalk

Powertalkers state their opinions directly. They do not look for consensus, approval, or agreement from others before they say what they think. (Or if they do, they are too smart to give it away by the way they make a declaration.)

Powertalkers project their opinions with confidence, and pursue them with tenacity. If others disagree, their tendency is not to backtrack, but to win them over.

The language of subtalkers, on the other hand, conveys a lack of confidence, because they are reluctant to possess an opinion which might be wrong. They reveal their tentativeness by using verbal devices which let them test the water with a toe before committing their whole foot. Submissive verbal devices give subtalk a wishy-washy quality, and make it hard to respect those who use it. We will take a closer look at subtalk devices—how to recognize them in yourself and how to free yourself of them—a little later in the chapter.

Powertalkers on the other hand, highlight their opinions by using a number of assertive verbal devices which I call *emphatics*.

Empathics
Strengthen Your Position

Emphatics throw out a challenge, and warn opponents that you are firm in your opinions and willing to fight for them. Other people, even those who are customarily quite assertive, will prick up their ears when they hear you use emphatics, and will quite literally move over to make room for you.

The Personal Stand Says You Stand Firm on What You Say

When you say "I" forcefully, you are taking a personal stand and putting all your power behind your statement. For instance: "*I* think you ought to pay the money back and apologize." (The emphasis is on the "I.")

When you place yourself squarely on the line and accept ownership for your opinions, you are practicing powertalk at its best. Notice how much stronger the speaker appears in the powertalk examples below than in the subtalk versions:

POWERTALK STATEMENT	SUBTALK STATEMENT
"*I* want more time."	"Most people would need more time."

"*I* want to implement it in stages."	"It might help if we implemented it in stages."
"*I* think the policy is wrong."	"There are those who believe the policy is wrong."
"*I'll* put my department on overtime."	"Someone's department will have to go on overtime."
"*My* reaction is different."	"There are different reactions to that."
"*I'm* in charge here."	"The organization chart indicates that the vice president in charge of operations is supervisor of this function."

The Voice of Authority Gives You the Right to Take Charge

When you haven't enough power on your own to make the personal stand effective, you can frequently "borrow" the power of a higher authority (a superior or an organization) by speaking as if you're the official voice of authority. For instance, when John Doe, clerk in the accounts receivable department, says to Mary Smith at IBM, "I want payment by the fifth or I'll have to take severe measures," she may not see the definite consequences. But when John Doe speaks for the telephone company and says, "*We* want payment by the fifth or we'll have to take severe measures," Mary may believe IBM's telephones will be cut off unless the check is mailed promptly.

Assistants use this tactic all the time to increase their power and establish small dictatorships. Look at the following examples: "Dr. Smith wants to see you now!". . . "The President says you can't attend the press conference.". . . "The Vice President wants me to be sure you stop using so many supplies; I expect a weekly usage report every Monday at ten."

You can even invoke vague higher authorities, such as, "Everyone knows Americans won't buy small cars.". . . "Secretaries always do the filing.". . . "Everyone else is cutting school on Friday."

When your position is essentialy powerless, authorities can be used to get what you want and build the foundations of a power base. However, the voice of authority can backfire on you. Powertalkers may well call your bluff by saying: "Let's go see what the Vice President has to say to me about this supply report nonsense." . . . "Who knows what Americans will buy?" . . . "I don't care what everyone else is doing, but you're going to school on Friday."

Absolutes Turn Simple Statements into Strong Ones

Absolutes like "always," "never," "all," and "none" strengthen statements. For instance: "Take your vitamins" is a strong, direct command. But "Always take your vitamins" is stronger as it applies to more than one event. And "Never skip your vitamins" is even more powerful, implying tremendous control over another's life and punitive action if disobeyed.

Other examples: "These ideas won't work" vs. "None of these ideas will work" (the latter makes it sound as if you have completely failed). "The doctors are busy" vs. "All the doctors are busy" (this sounds as if there are thousands of doctors scurrying around).

Moral Authority Is Psychological Manipulation

The word "should" has an invisible moral authority that lurks in everyone's superego. We've all been socialized by "shoulds," and only the best-analyzed of us have gotten even partially free of the reflexive guilt and compulsion after being told we should do something.

"Should" is most powerful when the force behind it remains mysterious. If you say "should" to someone who has the presence of mind to ask, "Says who?" your bluff has been called and you'll have trouble regaining your position. But few people use the right attack against a "should." Instead, if they ask anything at all, they say, "Why should I?" And that's easy to defend against—just find the "should" category that pushes their buttons (fear of mother, God, offending public opinion, or losing money are the most basic moral authorities). Don't be afraid to try a couple until you strike it lucky.

Here's how the word "should" works in a father/son conversation. Notice how many moral authorities are invoked until the right one works:

> SON: *You should lend me your car tonight, Dad.*
>
> FATHER: *Oh and just why should I?*
>
> SON: *Because Kenny's father lent him his.*
>
> FATHER: *What does that have to do with me?*
>
> SON: *Not only that but I'm going to look bad in front of Jennifer if we have to drive around with Kenny all night instead of having a car of my own.*
>
> FATHER: *If Jennifer is that shallow, she hardly seems worth pursuing.*
>
> SON: *And the other thing is that Kenny drinks too much, his car has lousy brakes, and it makes me nervous to drive with him.*
>
> FATHER: *All right, take the car, but God help you if there's so much as a scratch on it when you bring it back.*

"Should" is great powertalk but "really should" is not. The "really" qualifies the statement and weakens it. When you tell someone they "really should" do something, you're also giving them permission not to do it. "Really should" is not a command but a way of absolving yourself of the obligation to command. If you say, "You really should take your vitamins," the standard reply is, "Yes, I know I should but I really don't want to." (The conversation could then degenerate into pure subtalk when you reply, "Okay, but don't say I didn't warn you.")

"Really should" is just a sheep in wolf's clothing.

De-Emphasizers, the Opposite of Emphatics

There are a number of devices in our language which serve as de-emphasizers, the opposite of emphatics. Among these are tag questions, qualifiers, disclaimers, and fillers. Both powertalkers and subtalkers use de-emphasizers, but there is a big difference in the ways and the frequency of their use. Powertalkers make occasional strategic use of de-emphasizers to strengthen their positions (in ways which we'll see). Subtalkers, on the other hand, use de-emphasizers constantly. Their purpose is to weaken their own statements, so that they won't arouse opposition, criticism, or disagreement from others. They are also creating safety positions for themselves, so that in case they are opposed, they will have a ready path of retreat!

Tag Questions Cast Doubt on What You've Just Said

A tag question is a statement with a question tagged onto the end: "It's a nice day, *isn't it?*"

Tag questions are sometimes practical conversational tools, even for a strong powertalker. They serve to get conversations going or obtain confirmation of information about which you're uncertain (such as, "The party's from five to nine, isn't it?"). A powertalker may use a tag question to elicit information without revealing that he or she doesn't know it. For instance, if a powertalker isn't high enough in the power structure to receive advance knowledge of top-level staff changes, she could make a positive statement based on rumors she's heard, using a tag question to leave room to maneuver if she's wrong: "The president fired John Smith, didn't he?"

A tag question can also be used as a mild powertalk threat to manipulate someone into doing something you want them to do: "You're not going to eat that ice cream alone, are you?"

Tag questions can even become heavy powertalk threats: "That's not really the way you mean to be talking to me, is it?" Or in an emphatic way: "I think this is the last time we're going to let them get away with that nonsense, don't you?"

But there's a darker side to tag questions, which is the more common subtalk tactic that weakens statements and signals readiness to be dominated. Subtalk tags occur when the key statement forwards the speaker's own opinion, feeling, belief, or intention and the tag question indicates a willingness to retract the opinion if it's not acceptable. For instance: "That's a great painting, isn't it?" . . . "Reagan is turning out to be a remarkable leader, isn't he?" . . . "I really should quit my job, shouldn't I?" . . . "This wine isn't very good, don't you agree?"

These tag questions are the speaker's way of saying, "You're wiser or otherwise better than me so I'm putting myself forth tentatively for you to either approve or reject. If you reject my statements, I'll take them back at once and go along with you. Just don't reject *me*."

Tag questions can provide you with the opportunity to dominate by selectively approving or rejecting the speaker's statement until you mold his or her opinions and behavior to your liking. To see how tag questions can work against you, examine this scenario:

> HUSBAND: *I think it's a very nice house for us, don't you?*
> WIFE: *Nice! The house may be fine but the neighbors keep pigs and it's twenty-five miles to the children's school!*
> HUSBAND: *Well, I wasn't saying we should buy it. I just thought the house itself was rather nice. Naturally, it's out of the question for us, isn't it?*

The husband invited his wife to shape his opinion, and once she did, he quickly agreed with her. As the one in control, the wife can emphasize her power by concluding, "I don't see how you can separate a house from the neighborhood. You sure don't see things clearly." Or she can be kind and condescending: "Yes, it's too bad. The house alone was okay."

Qualifiers Are the Opposites of Absolutes___

Qualifiers can also be statement softeners but, while tag questions work by questioning the statement, qualifiers equivocate. Classic qualifiers are: "somewhat," "sort of," "well," "perhaps," "kind of," "a little," "I wonder." In the husband and wife example above, "rather" in "rather nice house" serves as a qualifier.

The addition of a qualifier weakens statements of opinions, softens the potential conflict with a dominant opponent, and prepares the way for a graceful retreat. Examples include:

POWERTALK STATEMENT	QUALIFIED (SUBTALK) STATEMENT
"You must never do that."	"*I don't think* you should ever do that."
"I don't want to."	"I don't *really* want to."

"I don't think it's a good idea."	"*Well*, I don't think it's a good idea."
"That's incorrect."	"That's *more or less* incorrect."
"I would like to."	"I *might* like to."
"That's strange."	"That's *somewhat* strange."
"Is that a good idea?"	"*I wonder if* that's a good idea?"
"No one ever does that."	"*Almost* no one ever does that."
"I like it."	"I *kind of* like it."
"I'm not certain."	"I'm *a little* uncertain."
"I'm sure."	"I'm *pretty* sure."
"I'm positive."	"I'm *fairly* positive."
"You're right."	"You're *probably* right."

Qualifiers are a much milder form of self-negation than self-questioning tags, and there are times when even the strongest powertalkers use them to soften blows or to genuinely equivocate the situations where they are unsure.

There are also ways in which qualifiers can be used deliberately by powertalkers to achieve certain power victories. When used sarcastically, for instance, they can put down another person and diminish another's win ("You're probably right," said in a tone of surprise or sarcasm when the other person is very right.)

Some qualifiers can be used to imply a threat if spoken in a heavy, slow, ominous tone. For example: "Well . . . I don't think it's a good idea" or "I wonder if that's a good idea" could both be very threatening, turning the tables on the other person and inviting him or her to back down.

Disclaimers Ask Forgiveness for What You're About to Say

Another form of statement softener, disclaimers "excuse" an expression of opinion, usually before any opinion is expressed. Sociologists John Hewitt and Randall Stokes have identified five different types of disclaimers:

1. **Suspension of judgment** is used to ward off emotional consequences: "*I don't want you to get mad but* I sold the dog."

2. **Cognitive disclaimers** are employed to avoid disbelief, ridicule, suspicions of poor logic, or nonpossession of the facts: "*This may sound crazy but* I hear the flowers talking to me." Or "*It's just off the top of my head but* I believe TV commercials are supposed to sell products."

3. **Sin licenses** explain or validate supposed misconduct or role-bending: "*This may violate the ordinary sense of the law, but not the spirit of these rules. . . .*" or "*While actually against the rules, we all know it's common practice to . . .*" or "*I know I should be in at eleven, Daddy dear, but since this was graduation night, I assumed . . .*"

4. **Credentialing** presents special attributes or qualities of the speaker when the reaction is expected to be negative or unfavorable: "*Some of my best friends are Martians, but* I still think green is a nutty color for . . ."

5. **Hedging** indicates the speaker is not adamant about his or her point but is willing to accept other views. It's also used when the speaker doesn't want to be held accountable for the statement and therefore hedges to avoid being diminished in the other's eyes: "*I could be mistaken but . . .*" "*I'm not entirely*

> *certain but . . ."* or *"I don't know how accurate she
> is, but* Mary did tell me . . ."

Disclaimers are a way of trying to have your conversational cake and eat it, too. They're used when you anticipate that another person is going to take issue with what you're about to say and you want to forestall this. When you use a disclaimer, you're telling the other person you know what you're about to say won't sound right, but you want to proceed anyway and would like to be heard out sympathetically.

In most cases, disclaimers are a particulary vicious kind of subtalk. The speaker thinks he or she is preparing for fair-minded judgment, but in fact, they signal the other person that you're feeling very submissive and give advance notice that your statement can be used against you.

Power people rarely need special dispensations from listeners. They're strong enough to look the other person straight in the eyes and say what's on their minds, relying on authority and charisma to support them and hold objections at bay.

There are few situations in which a powertalker employs disclaimers deliberately:

- If you're not in a position of strength and a disclaimer can help you forestall objections that might thwart you, you might be able to use a disclaimer to score a point which, once fully expressed, might speak for itself. For example: "I know you don't believe in letting employees take vacations in winter, boss, but I believe I'll be publicizing the company when I accept the award in person."

- If a fast reaction might reveal you had unauthorized advance information, a disclaimer can forestall any accusations, yet let you make a strong impression.

For example: "I know I haven't given this much thought, since you just announced a vacancy on the board, but how about appointing Frank?"

- Aggressive disclaimers turn the apology into a demand. For instance, suppose you want someone to lend you money but you know this friend has a strict principle against it. You anticipate your friend will answer your request with, "You know I never lend money. I think my friendships are too important to jeopardize in that way." You can force your friend to rethink his or her position and avoid an automatic refusal by starting with a disclaimer: "Listen Harvey, I know you have this thing about never lending money to friends, but right now I'm really in a tight spot and need you to make an exception for me." You might not get the loan, but you will certainly make it harder for Harvey to say no!

Fillers Help You Avoid Getting to the Point___

Pause words like "er," "um," "you know," "like," "it occured to me that," and "well . . ." are all space fillers—little verbal hiccups that serve to slow down concision. At times, this serves a valuable purpose or even adds powertalk intensity. But more often, fillers make you look slow, dull-witted, and confused. Only use fillers when you need to slow things down for a particular effect. For example:

- Everyone finds fillers helpful for creating time to think. But powertalkers use them with discretion and forethought, accompanying the filler with an air of solemnity to give the pause an aura of judicious, careful consideration. For instance, if the boss just stunned you by suggesting a 10 percent cut in your staff, the powertalk response would be to lean back, assume a serious expression, and murmur, "Yes, I see . . . now, let me think . . . well . . ." Subtalkers, on the other hand, would desperately sputter out a series of fillers (mostly "um" and "er," which are primarily subtalk fillers), appearing totally stunned and at a loss.

- Fillers can soften what might be taken as an unnecessarily authoritative or harsh statement. "That color, um, really doesn't look, er, so terrific on you" sounds kinder and warmer than, "That color really looks terrible on you."

- Fillers can change the level of conversation, making it either more formal or more colloquial. For example:
  DIRECT: "That would be difficult to do." (A challenge or hostile response depending on tone of voice and situation.)
  FORMAL: "Well, that would be, um, difficult to do." (A more ponderous statement that can ally you with those in authority by implying you share responsibility for the command just issued, or it can give someone a chance to back down. This is particularly effective with subordinates who are trying to powertalk up to you by putting forward a new idea.)
  COLLOQUIAL: "Yeah, well, that would be kind of difficult to do." (In most cases, this sounds like subtalk—a foot-dragging resistance without power behind it.)

- Fillers can also help test the waters before committing yourself to an opinion. By slowly saying, "Well, it sounds like a good idea, um . . ." while watching the other person carefully, you can determine his or her reaction before concluding the sentence with, "So let's do it." Be very careful to use this sparingly, however (and usually in situations where you're dealing with someone who has a great deal more power than you have), because changing your reaction to suit another is subtalk, even if you hide it this way. You can get away with disguised subtalk once or twice but not more often than that.

There's always a danger in using fillers of any kind in that they provide opportunities for others to break into your discussion time and steal the floor. Never use fillers in meetings where you aren't powerful enough to guarantee you won't be interrupted.

Subtalk fillers often become a nervous habit like a facial tic, flooding your conversation and drowning the impact of your statements. We've all seen TV interviews in which the man (or woman) on the street inserts "you know" or a similar filler between every second or third word. You may have found this funny, but you probably also felt annoyance, lost track of the conversation, and concluded the person was semiliterate. Break any filler habits you may have developed immediately!

Powertalkers not only use fillers with deliberate forethought for specific objectives but they use them very sparingly. If your conversation is peppered with fillers, you're subtalking. And the best way to get over such automatic usage is to cut fillers out entirely for several months.

Opinions Are More Convincing When Buttressed with Facts

When talking for amusement or pleasure, imaginative, individual language is not only acceptable but desirable. However, the language of power is neither innovative nor colorful. Instead, it's as factual and descriptive as possible. Why? The answer goes back to power. Power deals with responsibility and obligation, with controlling people, building things, and acquiring and protecting property. These preoccupations are naturally expressed in language that's very factual and employs precise description.

Power strives for absolute clarity so there can be no mistaking what's wanted. The language of power tries to be complete so there's no room to maneuver. (Unfortunately, these two needs often collide, resulting in legal language and the complex jargon used in bureaucracy and areas like education.) Expressive and interpretive language is traditionally a part of art, culture, and personal sensibilities—all of which have always been relegated to those without real power or property.

The factual, descriptive language of power says this is the way things are. The expressive, interpretive language of the powerless says this is how things seem to the person speaking. The first is presumably objective and takes authority from its claim to reality. The latter is subjective and has the weakness associated with matters of sensibility and individual opinion.

Journalists have long recognized the power of the seemingly objective viewpoint to convince. That's why newspapers stick to the facts and reserve opinions for the editorial page. Although many sophisticated readers realize that newspapers express highly personal opinions through selection of priorities and presentation of facts, the overall appearance seems unbiased—making it far more effective an influence than editorials.

Politicians, those other master manipulators of opinion, also present selected facts and edited history as if they were objective reality. Even scientists camouflage opinions as research findings. There's a well-known book entitled *How to Lie with Statistics*, which proves that not even figures are totally complete and unbiased.

Powertalkers present opinions because they want to convince others to agree with them. Buttressing your opinion statements with facts and removing the subjective elements can make you far more influential. For example: A nuclear engineer acting as a spokesman for a power company argues for building a plant at a contested waterfront site. Which argument is more convincing?

> POWERTALK: *"Cooling will be carried out by a circulating heat-transfer system which allows no contact between cooling water and any radioactive contaminants. The water will be returned to the bay at 78°F. Far from causing ecological harm, studies at the Johns Point and Harris Bay plants indicate this provides a warm-water refuge for fish that actually improves local sport fishing."*
>
> SUBTALK: *"I don't think you have any need to worry about radiation in the discharged water. And as far as water temperature is concerned, it will only be a little warmer than usual. The fish will probably love it."*

The power of this language is so widely acknowledged that now areas which used to be the land of the powerless and vague are developing special factual languages! Today, for example, wine connoisseurs say, "This wine has a good nose and a true, rich, ruby color" rather than, "I really like this wine; it tastes good, smells like flowers, and the color reminds one of the rich tapestries of medieval days." Most areas of the arts, in fact, now use special descriptive languages (called jargon) that permit critics to express feelings and interpretations in a factual and technical manner.

Tape Your Conversations to See How You Express Opinions

The use of emphatics, de-emphasizers, and factual language is often so automatic that you may not be aware of precisely what you're saying and how often. The best way to analyze your conversation is to tape yourself in various situations (since you may use powertalk in one area of your life and subtalk in another), then evaluate the frequency of your use of fillers, disclaimers, personal stands, etc.

If you find that you're subtalking, create actual exercises for yourself. Practice expressing opinions in factual language by speaking out loud as you drive your car, for example. Decide you are going to stop using fillers and make a conscious effort to do so, listening to yourself with awareness whenever possible. Make an effort to add one emphatic at a time to your language by using it as often as possible over a period of a few weeks. Every month, tape yourself again and examine your progress until you're satisfied.

This is important because until you can express opinions forcefully, positively, and confidently, you cannot really powertalk. In powertalk workshops, I create role-playing situations for people, tape them, and then let them listen to the tapes. The experience is frequently a revelation to many people.

One extremely bright and well-educated young woman was having trouble getting a suitable job, so I created an interviewing situation for her, and taped it. When she listened to the tape, she was amazed to hear, not the self-assured, assertive person she thought of herself as being, but someone who was hesitant, self-apologetic, and obviously eager to please. She was not an unatrractive or unemployable person, but certainly not someone you would think of for a high-level management post.

With my coaching and encouragement she winnowed all of the subtalk mannerisms out of her language and replaced them with decisive emphatics. We taped the same exercise two more times, and by the final tape she sounded so mature and sure of herself that you would not believe it was the same person. She soon began receiving offers for much better jobs, and was employed within a month.

Summary

Expressing opinions often separates the powertalker from the subtalker. Powertalkers are direct because they don't need the approval of others to validate them. In fact, powertalkers deliberately express opinions as strongly as possible in order to convince others to agree with them. Subtalkers believe a direct, clear statement of opinion will expose their weaknesses to attack or rejection and often signal a readiness to withdraw their statements before they even finish speaking.

Powertalkers use emphatics to strengthen their statements:

- The personal stand stresses the word "I" and puts your personal power and authority behind the statement.

- The voice of authority "borrows" the power of a higher authority by stating that you speak officially on the authority's behalf.

- Absolutes like "always" and "never" strengthen statements by making them apply to more than one situation.

- The moral authority of "should" pushes an inner psychological button but "really should" is a subtalk weakener.

Subtalkers use a range of de-emphasizers to weaken their statements (powertalkers use the same devices but in deliberate ways on rare occasions for specific purposes):

- Tag questions are tagged onto the end of a statement to indicate a willingness to withdraw a statement of the speaker's opinion, feeling, belief, or intention.

- Qualifiers are words or phrases that equivocate a statement (as in "I'm pretty sure").

- Disclaimers "excuse" an expression of opinion.

- Fillers are verbal hiccups used to slow down concision and should be used only with great care: It's easy to develop a "filler habit," and you should be very sure to uncover any habit you may have and break it.

Powertalkers use factual and technically descriptive language to sound more authoritative and objective. They avoid descriptive, interpretative, or imaginative language, which is considered subjective and weak.

POWER WORDS
FROM POWER WORLDS
4

Let's look at another aspect of the language which clearly separates the powertalkers from the subtalkers—the vocabulary they use. Although powertalk and subtalk both use the same language, each draws its own distinctive vocabulary from it. The separation occurs because words have hidden meanings, special connotations that go beyond their definitions. Writers know this and strive to find the words with the emotional overtone that create specific feelings. By choosing words carefully, they can create moods and reveal a lot of information without extensive exposition.

For instance, the thesaurus lists luxurious, elegant, plushy, and extravagant as synonyms having similar meanings. However, luxurious has a sensuous tone to it—a rich man's mistress might have a luxurious boudoir. Elegant seems very wealthy. A proper Bostonian might have an elegant home, but never a plush home—plush is better suited to the ornate overkill of a janitor-turned-millionaire lottery winner. And extravagant makes you think of someone who goes overboard.

As a powertalker, you can use these supplemental meanings in power encounters. For instance, suppose you're at a party in a newly decorated home and while sparring for power with someone you've just met, he or she says, "Isn't this an elegant home?"

"Yes," you answer, "it's quite extravagant."

Extravagant? your opponent thinks, suddenly very uneasy. Is it overdone? Is there something wrong with my taste? Has our host spent too much? I do business with him—can I trust him with my money? By using one word, in this instance, you've put your opponent off guard and won an advantage.

These nuances also tell people a great deal about who you are. Very different kinds of people use different words to express the same thing—auto, car, wheels, jalopy, and buggy, for example. By using the right words, you can upgrade your social status in someone's eyes, convey authority, become a member of the "in" group, demonstrate your expertise in a technical area, reveal that you keep up with the times, tell your age, hint at your ancestry, and more.

Powertalkers deliberately choose words to create impressions, gain ascendancy over people, and to lend force to their communications. In fact, powertalkers use vocabulary in three ways:

1. They choose powertalk words over subtalk words. Powertalk words convey force, authority or leadership either directly or because of their connotations and source (from an arena of power).

2. They choose a specific vocabulary appropriate to a particular type of leader in order to play a role that people recognize as powerful. During difficult power struggles with important stakes (getting ahead in business, for example), powertalkers will adopt a

role and the vocabulary of that role in order to make opponents uneasy, force subordinates to submit, or impress higher authorities. For instance, they may take on the vocabulary of the head of the company, or a known general or politician.

3. They choose specific words from either the powertalk or subtalk vocabularies to influence others or cast doubts on the abilities of opponents.

MANTALK, WOMANTALK

I do not wish to offend people by seeming sexist, but the truth is that for the most part words from masculine domains have power connotations, while words from feminine domains do not. Masculine and feminine are the most basic classifications of powerful and powerless language.

As women come to power in more and more areas that were once the solid bastions of men, these distinctions will become less sex-oriented, but for now power words come from masculine fields. Just remember that I don't want it that way, and I didn't make it that way.

The classic areas of male interest are warfare and military, contact sports, banking, finance, heavy industry, manufacturing, architecture, construction, hard sciences, space, engineering, mathematics, law, accounting, and big business. Words from all these areas have become accepted in the common descriptive vocabulary of powertalk.

The classic female domains are the home, motherhood, decorating, crafts, menial service and support jobs (secretary, receptionist, nurse, dental hygenist, early childhood education, librarian, etc.). Words from these "female" occupations and interests are low in power and therefore subtalk. In addition, words that are imagistic—those concerned with feelings, sensations, aesthetics, nature, psychology, and moral/ethical philosophies—are generally subtalk.

Subtalk Vocabularies

The following is a preliminary list of feminine words that signal submission, deference, and low power:

1. **Homemaking:** Neaten, spruce up, simmer, mend, dust, messy, mop, decorate, touch up, shine up, straighten up, house clean, dart, shirr, baste, braise, crochet, knit, unravel.

   Because they're more active or are used in other, more "masculine" activities as well, the following words are not subtalk: Scrub (medical association saves it), boil, broil, roast, steam, straight out, clear out or clear up.

2. **Nurturing:** Nurture, nourish, care, reassure, feed, baby, nap, playroom, playschool, nursery, cuddly, pat, paddle, bawl, cranky, whiny, naughty.

3. **Aesthetics:** Shade, hue, mauve, beige, rosy, harmonize, decor, chic, stylish, acquamarine, taupe (all kinds of unusual and subtle color variations).

4. **Personal Qualities:** Chatter, nag, gossip, bitch, scatterbrain, picky, fussy, gabby, rapport, lively, warmth, sensitive, timid, shy, graceful, engaging.

5. **Feelings and Perceptions:** Feelings, relate, goodness, precious, adorable, cute, pretty, charming, terribly, awfully, fabulous, marvelous (hyperbole generally).

As a general rule, subtalk includes almost all adverbs, adjectives that relate to emotion or sensitivity, and nouns and verbs which originated in activities that used to be considered "women's work."

Here are some examples of how the use of the right words can change the power potential of a sentence:

SUBTALK	POWERTALK
"I cut down his ideas."	"I demolished his ideas."
"We'll have to mend that break."	"We'll have to repair that break."
"We're gossiping about staff changes."	"We're discussing staff changes."
"I don't want to nag you."	"I don't want to remind you."
"You're very gabby."	"You're very articulate."
"We're going to clean this department up."	"We're going to strip this department bare."
"He's a very nurturing, supportive ally."	"He's a good team player."

Notice that you can use subtalk descriptive words to cast aspersions on opponents in power struggles. If, for example, you and a coworker were both up for promotion, you could do a lot of damage by describing your opponent with subtalk—such as "he chatters" vs. "he's talkative." Or "he's picky" vs. "he pays attention to detail."

Stealing from the Specialists

The colorful parts of the powertalk vocabulary are borrowed from specialized areas such as sports, construction, and business. For example:

1. **Sports:** Scrimmage, knockout, huddle, pitch, lineup, touchdown, jab, ringside, home run, etc. The most powerful words are from the most com-

petitive physical sports like boxing, football and, to a lesser extent, baseball. Words from betting sports such as horseracing also have power.

2. **War and Military:** War games, strategy, maneuver, protect your flanks, bring up the big guns, rear-guard action, skirmish, battle zone, front line, troops, advance, strategic retreat, launch, CO, battle plan, plan of attack, headquarters, enemy camp, infiltrate, tactics, spy out the terrain, good soldier.

3. **Money:** Bottom line, in the red, in the black, annuity, dividend, asset, money in the bank, a little cushion, net, etc. When referring to money, power-talk implies familiarity with big numbers: "10 mil," 30 K," "per M," "60 thou," "100 C's." In some discussions, the hundreds or thousands are dropped to indicate these are small numbers to the power-talker. For example: "It'll cost you six." Or "I got my house for under 450."

When the words of high finance are applied to your personal financial situation, you increase your status, imply greater wealth, and downplay your money problems. Just look at how different the right phrases make you look:

SUBTALK (ACTUAL SITUATION)	POWERTALK (HIGH-FINANCE WORDS)
"I'm broke."	"I'm experiencing a negative cash flow."
"My deposit hasn't cleared."	"The bank is playing with the float."
"I'm deeply in debt."	"I'm extremely well leveraged."

"I can't pay you until I get my tax refund check."

"My receivables are very late pay recently."

"Everything I've got in the world is in a savings and checking account."

"My assets are handled by my banker."

"I take my taxes to H&R Block."

"My accountant handles my finances."

"I'll pay you out of my next paycheck."

"I've already allocated resources to take care of you."

4. **Industrial, Construction, Labor:** Demolish, takeover, outbid, erect, produce, assembly line, package, exploit, reinforce, maximize, rollout, analyze, buttress, frame, on the line, roll off the line, slowdown, downtime, let out the clutch, throw in reverse, gun the motor, give it some gas (or juice), clear the pipes, etc.

5. **Crime and Violence:** Hold-up, stick-up, at gunpoint, gun to my head, a steal, robbing me blind, rape (used in negotiating and setting prices).

6. **Assorted Specialties:** Trucker and CB terms, police terms, politics and international diplomacy terms (coup, detente, palace revolution, spheres of interest).

Buzzwords Show You're Up to Date _____

Buzzwords are power people's unique slang—they're dropped as soon as everyone else starts using them. Buzzwords come from new discoveries and events that are exciting and carry the aura of power. The first people to use a buzzword gain power because they evoke an electrifying image. The next group of people who use the new word don't gain or lose power—they simply show they're part of the power "in" group. The people who continue to use a buzzword (or worse yet, start) after the word has been adopted by everyone else lose power because they show they don't know what language the power circles are using.

Because of the way buzzwords work, any words I mention now are sure to be outdated by the time you read this book. "Cutting edge" and "up-to-speed" are two buzzwords that worked their way into accepted powertalk. "Fast track" is another. But "stonewall," "clone," and "synergy" are now subtalk. Space words were hot items as buzzwords for a while; computer terms like "update," "master program," and others are half generally accepted powertalk and half buzzwords.

As I write, power people have picked up on a phrase coming out of Hollywood—"my people" ("put my people in touch with your people"). And in keeping with the interest in the economy, they've adopted a few of the government's terms for the national economic situation. But by the time you read this, there are apt to be a whole new set of buzzwords. Keep your ears open when you're around power people!

Talking to Specialists in Their Lingo

Whenever special training or technical expertise is required, a special sublanguage develops called jargon (which is officially defined as obscure and often pretentious language marked by circumlocutions and long words). Specialists are rarely powerful people; leaders in industry, government, and other areas of life pride themselves on being generalists who can "see the big picture" and put down specialists as technicians who are "caught up in the details and can't see the forest for the trees." That's why jargon is helpful to powertalkers only in limited situations. For example:

1. When talking to specialists, use their lingo if you

can do so correctly. You lose more power by misusing jargon in these situations than you can gain by using it. You gain power by indicating to specialists that you've done your homework and can't be hoodwinked. By using powertalk from outside their sphere of interest in addition to their jargon, you also tell specialists that you know more than they do.

2. Avoid low-power specialist or bureaucratic jargon, particularly when speaking to someone who is not a specialist. Much of this jargon is subtalk, avoiding the personal stand and other powertalk elements, and often it sounds pompous and boring. You could be "demoted" by speaking it (your opponent might conclude you're part of this low-power world).

3. Jargon from high-power specialties constitute an exception which can enhance your power image. Medical terms, high-level scientific terms, and high-technology terms all carry some of the power of these specialties.

4. Jargon that's fun and unique can occasionally become a fad among power people, used to show they're aware of many areas of life and "with it." Like buzzwords, the style passes very quickly, once the fun is over. But for a while, CB talk, for example, was used at all levels of power.

5. Jargon that provides a real benefit to power people can be adopted quickly. This is especially true of jargon that softens very negative impacts on subordinates—"deficit spending," for instance, and "rolling readjustments" in place of "a boom or bust economy." Since those who speak for big business to the public or shareowners constantly seek such

"softeners" to deliver bad news, use of these terms hints that you have enough power to function in this capacity.

Big Words: Be Careful

Talking like an academic intellectual is dangerous in the power world. Even powerful people are quick to put down and even mock what they don't understand. Using big words can make you seem more intelligent and better educated with some people and give you a power advantage (usually those who are easily intimidated by education). But big words frequently backfire—self-made power people without formal education are particularly prone to ruthless attack at the least sign of superior education.

Weapon Words Can Work for or Against You

Weapon words are those aspects of language that can be very helpful or very hurtful, depending on how you use them and how well you understand the rules of power. Consider the following:

1. **Double-edged words can mean two things.** Words that describe accurately but have destructive connotations are extremely effective forms of powertalk in situations where you're engaged in long-term, cutthroat power struggles. For example:

YOU SAY ...	OTHERS UNDERSTAND YOU TO SAY ...
"She does an honest job."	"Honest but it lacks . . ."
"That's nice."	"Nice" means not great, not even particularly good, just acceptable.

"He's hyperactive."	"He's constantly in aimless motion that accomplishes nothing."
"She's skinny."	"Too thin" rather than svelte or slim.
"That's a fancy idea."	Often means "too complicated and elaborate, not practical."

2. **Diminutives are usually weakeners.** Describing people with diminutives robs them of power, calling attention to shortcomings and implying a condescending attitude that clearly established the speaker as more powerful. For example:

YOU SAY ...	OTHERS UNDERSTAND YOU TO SAY ...
"He's the cutest little man."	A very clear put-down
"She's one hell of a little woman."	Praise that also puts down a person as a woman
"He's a little powerhouse."	Praise that highlights size

3. **Humor is rarely powertalk.** Extremely powerful people do tell jokes but since subordinates *must* laugh, such humor is frequently an exercise of power prerogatives or a lesson to remind subordinates that they're submissive. A powertalker may even *command* the appropriate response by beginning, "You'll die when you hear this . . ." or "You'll love this story."

Powertalkers don't like to listen to other people's jokes, however, because they're forced to act submissively, remaining silent and paying attention to you. A joke during a power struggle may even be a tactic to gain the upper hand.

Avoid humor except with peers and always avoid self-deprecating humor (for instance: "I did the silliest thing yesterday . . .")—that's pure subtalk.

4. **Slang is a generational jargon that establishes your age group.** If you ever lie about your age, watch your slang—it can be a dead giveaway! Powertalkers speak very little slang. They may occasionally use a mild phrase from their own generation's slang to establish an in-group atmosphere (for instance, if someone very young has achieved a lot of power and authority, older power people may close ranks to exclude the newcomer by speaking their slang). Power people also pick up on slang that can work as weapon words. For example:

> **SAYING IT STRAIGHT:** *"I know you have a strong principle against lending money to friends but . . ."*
> **SAYING IT WITH SLANG:** *"I know you have 'this thing' against lending money to friends but . . ." (The slang makes the principle sound like an eccentricity.)*

Another Example:

> **YOU SAY:** *"My hobby is breeding horses. In fact, I've got one ready for the Kentucky Derby."*
> **POWERTALKER INTERRUPTS:** *"Oh yes, I heard you were 'into' horses." (Trivializes an interest that could be a strong power base.)*

Since slang requires you to adopt language created by someone else, it's generally more subtalk than powertalk.

5. **Proverbs and clichés work both ways.** Powertalkers are concerned that others understand in-

structions clearly, so they do employ clichés because there's rarely any confusion over what they
mean. However, powertalkers take proverbs and
clichés only from the power language of military,
sports, finance, business, construction, etc. "A
stitch in time" and other phrases associated with
women and "women's work" are subtalk.

Ethnic proverbs that almost every nationality
uses to convey folk wisdom are also subtalk, possibly because they originated as a verbal teaching
technique for the unschooled and were used primarily by women.

Powertalk Swearing

The use of obscenities, profanity, and euphemisms
("nice" words in place of the "bad" ones) is complex.

Generally, the dominant person in a group determines
how dirty the language will be. Subtalkers use obscenities only after the leader does (unless they're rebelling,
inviting a power struggle, or asking for a put-down).
However, once obscenities are used, people often compete
to be a little dirtier than everyone else, and unless the
leader exercises some controls, the language quickly de-
generates.

In a middle-level power position, your best bet is to
follow the leader. If you don't swear (especially if you use
a lot of euphemisms) while everyone else is cursing like
mad, you look prissy. If you sound off like an old-time
sailor while everyone else is saying "golly" and "gee," you
look like a lowlife. Both images cause a loss of status, and
swearing leaves you open to a sharp reprimand that's
tough to counter.

No matter what your power position, limit your own
use of profanity. You're not out to win a cursing competition, and when obscenities are seldom used, they have
greater impact. If it's extremely unusual for you to use
harsh language, you can get away with it even in the

presence of a very powerful non-cursing leader. Sudden use of a strong obscenity can also escalate a power struggle or attack an opponent.

Euphemisms, on the other hand, are subtalk, communicating that you can't deal with things directly. The few euphemisms used by powertalkers come from strong power sources (such as "head" from the military).

Don't Memorize Words — Concentrate on the Principles

Don't make an effort to memorize the words mentioned in this chapter. Focus on learning the basic principles underlying powertalk vocabularies and you'll find that you automatically begin to use the right words.

Summary

The rules of vocabulary are simple:

1. Powertalk words come from the power areas of life—money, finance, big business, construction, and he-man activities like contact sports and warfare. Subtalk words come from what used to be the "feminine" areas of life as well as the fields of art and aesthetics.

2. Obscure sublanguages used by specialists (jargon) are best used with specialists. Don't try to speak any sublanguage perfectly—whether it's jargon, preppie, or old power. Aim at using the sublanguage well enough to make the person you're talking to feel comfortable.

3. Use buzzwords only if you pick them up very fast; don't be a follower.

4. Watch out for humor, proverbs, slang, and profanity—when in doubt, don't.

THE
POWERTALK
DELIVERY

5

In the last chapters, you've learned how powertalkers say what they think, and what words they use. These elements combine to project a good part of the image of a person who is accustomed to being a leader. However, this image will ring false unless the details of delivery are right. Just as an actor perfects the nonverbal nuances of a role—the gestures, mannerisms, and movements—people who change their verbal styles should pay attention to the nonverbal nuances of their role.

The actor/director Mike Nichols used to do a sketch that demonstrated the importance of projecting a part. Portraying a macho Southern writer lecturing to a women's club, he would swagger into the hall, shirt unbuttoned to the navel, glance insolently at the audience, deal out his index cards like they were a hand at poker, and then after another long, insolent glance, suddenly simper, "Ladies." It always brought the house down.

So now we are going to improve your delivery of powertalk . . . the way you use your voice and body. The follow-ing are some of the reasons for (and benefits of) mastering these techniques:

1. Powertalk and subtalk have very different sounds and body positions. With the former, you give off an air of command and assurance. With the latter, you appear timid and used to taking orders rather than giving them. It's almost impossible to powertalk ef-fectively while using subtalk sounds and body posi-tions.

2. Your delivery style makes an enormous impact on issuing clearly understood instructions and direc-tions. It can also aid in getting ideas and projects accepted.

3. In power struggles, your body language and delivery can be used deliberately to add emphasis, put your opponents off guard, intensify meanings without committing yourself to them, and more. A very basic example is the yes/no sexual innuendo: A coworker leans across a desk creating intimacy with his body language, stares at the woman's chest and in a low, husky voice, says, "That's a great sweater."

   If the woman correctly interprets the nonverbal lan-guage and reacts as if the man has not commented on her clothing, the man pulls back in astonished innocence, replying, "I was just commenting on your new outfit! Just what did you think I was talking about?"

This nonverbal aspect of powertalk is easy to learn if you think of yourself as an actor playing the role of a very powerful person—perhaps a president. You'll be surprised at how automatically you pick up the sound and move-ment of powertalk!

Turn Your Voice Into A Powertalk Instrument

Research studies have proven that people attach certain qualities to vocal characteristics. Based on these alone, they even make very firm judgments about people's personalities, morals, social status, etc. Using this research, it's posible to define powertalk and subtalk voices quite distinctly.

I frequently run into people who have been held back in life by a tone of voice or style of delivery that belies rather than reinforces their considerable, innate authority.

One of the brightest and most creative women I have ever worked with had a high-pitched, whiny voice that made her sound like an unhappy child all of the time. She was in the magazine business and could always find employment writing and doing copy editing, but could never make the break into the senior editorial ranks where she would be taking on administrative and policy responsibilities, despite her obvious talents. With that voice, especially on the business end of the magazine, people just weren't willing to take her seriously.

Sometimes the roots of a self-effacing voice and delivery are deep in a personality. The woman in my example had an overall reluctance to be an adult and take on all of the responsibilities that go with it. These attitudes took an increasingly high toll as she grew older, until finally she developed a real motivation to change and entered therapy. Even with therapy, however, her vocal delivery didn't change spontaneously, but required specific attention. Finally, when she was in her late thirties, she moved to a new magazine, where she got a chance to do the caliber of work for which she was qualified.

Another client of mine was a talented illustrator who was trained to be an art director. His work was consistently clever and sharp, but when he was asked his opinion about how an idea should be illustrated, he would say something vague like, "I dunno, you could do it in a lot of ways, I guess," and then he would let his voice mumble off at the end of the sentence.

At first meeting, people just thought of him as some sort of dolt, but after seeing his rather brilliant and decisive portfolio, they revised their opinion to one of a talented eccentric, but still one who had to be kept in the back room behind the drawing board.

After he learned to speak out with a good powertalk delivery, and to hazard a firm opinion, he began to move out of the back room, and eventually he did get a job that he wanted as an art director.

VOLUME

The sound of authority is slightly loud but relaxed, without shouting. Before microphones took over the acting profession, theater people were trained to project their voices so they could be heard in the back of the balcony even when whispering. This is how powertalkers speak.

Projection isn't hard to learn. You increase the loudness of your voice without changing pitch or quality (normally, you speak higher and more harshly when you shout). It's hard to hear whether you're projecting or slipping into shouting by yourself—so practice with a friend standing across the room to listen to you and advise you.

Subtalkers speak either too soft or too loud. The soft voice is easy to understand; they're afraid to be too authoritative. The loud voice is also due to insecurity; it's an effort to compensate for inferiority feelings or a result of years of not being listened to. Subtalkers also don't control shifts from loud to soft well. They tend to change at inappropriate times or become steadily louder the longer they speak in a vain effort to close out interruptions.

Powertalkers keep their voices at an even volume, reserving shouting for an extreme threat or intimidation. Occasionally, powertalk masters will demonstrate their power over subordinates by speaking so softly that everyone is forced to lean forward in a reverent, semi-bowed position and maintain absolute silence. This doesn't work when talking to other powertalkers who will take advantage of the difficulty in hearing to override the speaker.

PITCH

Pitch is the level of your voice (soprano, alto, tenor, baritone, and bass are the musical terms for the major voice pitches). Our culture prefers a low-pitched voice for both men and women. As advertisers have proven repeatedly in scientific tests, a low voice conveys assurance and relaxed authority. All of us tend to believe that people with high-pitched voices are immature, strident, or slightly hysterical.

It's possible to shift the pitch of your voice. Many actors have done so successfully. Although a vocal coach is the best way to do this, there are books to help you do it yourself. If you have a very high-pitched voice, it might well be worthwhile.

In addition to basic pitch, powertalkers don't vary the pitch of their voices as much as subtalkers. They speak at a level that gives the impression that they're always in control and never ruled by emotion. They reserve variations in pitch for specific situations when they need the emotional overtones to win a point. Subtalkers may overuse pitch variations to try to hold attention and emphasize. In doing so, they often end up sounding excessively dramatic.

SPEED

Powertalkers take their time. Although people speak at different speeds in different parts of the country (for instance, city dwellers speak faster, Southerners speak much more slowly than the average), powertalkers generally speak slightly slower than the average rate of speed in their area. This gives their speech a sense of seriousness and careful deliberation. As with pitch, powertalkers also tend to speak at a steady speed rather than changing the rate frequently. Speed shifts are used to deliver specific messages—a slowdown is for threat or intimidation; a speed-up means it's time to conclude a meeting or discussion or that the powertalker is annoyed.

Subtalkers either vary speed inappropriately or speak faster than the average, trying to finish before someone interrupts.

BREATH

The amount of breath in a voice makes it husky (breathy) or sharp (very little breath). A husky voice that includes many pauses for breath is subtalk. People think of this kind of voice as shallow, overeager, and young. Powertalkers speak with a *slightly* breathy voice, but you don't notice them breathing (unless they're using breathing as a way to pause or intensify). This may be part of the reason why powertalkers keep sentences short. They *never* run out of breath in the middle of a sentence and gasp.

RHYTHM

There's a certain rhythm to good speech. Think of John F. Kennedy's inaugural address or any of Martin Luther King, Jr.'s speeches and you'll instantly recall their almost musical rhythms. Orators use rhythm consciously because it catches attention, makes the content memorable, and stirs emotion. Although the broad, obvious rhythms of an orator would be pretty ridiculous in everyday conversation, powertalk often has a definite beat that makes it sound more coherent and assured.

Powertalk is also smooth, flowing along with only deliberate pauses and hesitations to emphasize key points. Subtalk, by contrast, tends to be jerky, uneven, and without the consistency that makes powertalk sound important.

The best powertalkers always sound a bit as if they'd rehearsed beforehand. And in a way, they do exactly that. By speaking slowly and not racing to leap into every gap in conversation, powertalkers give themselves enough time to think about what they're about to say so they can speak smoothly, evenly, and coherently. To keep your voice under control, don't rush; think before you speak and stay cool.

Your Accent: Use It or Lose It? _____

People judge accents. At times this creates an obstacle for powertalkers, and at other times it works to their advantage. Does your accent help or hinder you? If the people you want to impress seem to like your accent, or at least feel at home with it, keep it. But if they prejudge it to your disadvantage, get rid of it!

It's impossible to analyze every possible accent, but the following guide will help to determine how people perceive yours.

ACCENT	HOW PEOPLE VIEW IT
Boston/Harvard	Highly educated, upper crust (unless it's very strong Boston with no Harvard overtones), overly intellectual in some circles.
British	Efficient, intelligent, perhaps associated with nobility. (At one time, secretaries with British accents were considered the ultimate status symbol for power people.)
Brooklyn	Low class, uneducated, street smarts.

French	Sexy, sophisticated, not quite moral.
German	Rigid, organized, unemotional.
"Red Neck," "Hillbilly" or "Cracker"	Uneducated, unintelligent, low class, highly conservative.
Regional British (Liverpool, Cockney, Manchester)	See "Red Neck."
Southern	Old family but decadent, slow (and sometimes educated).
Texas	Prone to exaggeration but exciting to be around, pioneer type, not overly intellectual, big bucks.
Western (USA)	Pioneer type, outdoors person, generous.

Even accents that are not well thought of generally can be effective at times. Labor leaders and politicians, for instance, may intensify their accents to reassure their constituencies. And the "old country boy" lawyer who's as clever as they come is so successful at using his accent that he's become a stock TV character. Even when an accent can work for you, some powertalkers prefer to be in control of theirs so they can use them to best advantage when they see fit.

All this is not to say you should adopt an accent you didn't come by naturally. That's risky because people are rarely as successful at imitating accents as they think they are. In addition, you run the danger of dropping out of character at a critical moment and giving the whole show away. You can certainly play with the accent you have, easing up or intensifying to suit your audience, but don't try to become someone else!

Enunciate to Avoid Being Classed As a Subtalking Mumbler

Enunciating or pronouncing words so they can be clearly understood is critical in powertalk because if no one understands you, you won't gain power. Mumbling is pure subtalk, a sign that the speaker is afraid to speak out straight. Extremely pedantic, careful pronunciation is also subtalk, indicating you're frequently misunderstood and taking special pains.

Powertalkers speak clearly but naturally. Sometimes they use extra careful pronunciation to show irritation and/or issue a mild threat (for example, switching from "You'll do this now, won't you?" to a slow, very careful, low-pitched, "You will do this now, will you not?").

A "Poker Face" and Lots of Eye Contact Are Powertalk

Subtalkers reveal their submissiveness by averting their heads to avoid eye contact, smiling frequently and inappropriately, and using many, often exaggerated, facial expressions. All this completely gives away the subtalker's eagerness to please, fear of offending, deference, and anxiety about holding the attention of an audience.

Powertalkers work to maintain eye contact but give away very little with facial expressions. Eye contact is important because it's a mild threat of dominance and also establishes a link that fixes attention. Powertalkers use intense eye contact in difficult power struggles or when they very much want to get an idea or instruction across because a locking glance excludes everyone but the two people looking at each other and creates a powerful bond. (The person to break off such a "lock" is usually submitting or on the verge of doing so unless a reason is established for breaking away, such as responding to the summons of another.)

Powertalkers play the eye contact game to the fullest. At times, they withhold eye contact quite deliberately. For example, when you meet a master powertalker at a party, he or she may barely acknowledge the introduction and continue scanning the room—a challenge tactic or a signal that the powertalker doesn't consider you worth knowing.

A colleague of mine who is a Zen therapist, makes brilliant use of this combination of a poker face and sustained eye contact. Whenever he suspects his clients are being less than totally honest with themselves and him, which, of course, is almost all of the time, he looks at them with an unblinkingly enigmatic smile that suggests he sees all, forgives it, and finds it an amusing part of the human comedy. Faced with this smile, they go through an amazing progression of claims, counterclaims, rationalizations, excuses, self-justifications, emotional outbreaks, confessions, and pleas for forgiveness until finally they strip away all the false levels of personality and reach bedrock.

I never did find out whether he really sees through them in the first place, or whether he just intuitively picks up the subtalk of self-deception, and simply keeps on staring until their voices sound more authentic. But whichever it is, the results are fantastic.

Withholding eye contact could also mean a powertalker has made a negative and final decision regarding you. For instance, an employer who won't establish eye contact with an employee who's been called in for a private meeting may be about to fire the employee. A lover who refuses to make eye contact may be saying that the romance is over, or trying to show anger he or she can't discuss but which is still important.

Lack of eye contact could also indicate what the speaker is saying is not true. For instance, if after a fight, one spouse pleads, "Honey, do you forgive me?" and the other says, "Of course I do" but won't meet the first spouse's eyes, the message could really be that the subject is far from closed and only a temporary truce exists.

Despite all this game-playing with eye contact, powertalkers use less facial expression than the average person. The expressionless face is an enigma, giving nothing away of the speaker's inner thoughts, turmoils, or plans. And if expression is used rarely, each change becomes more important to the audience. Cultivate a poker face as part of your powertalk delivery. Practice downplaying your expressions, using less than the average person. Focus on using expression to communicate your intentions and be especially stingy about using expression to respond to anything other people say (since active response, whether vocal or merely expressive, enhances the power of the speaker).

Powertalkers Also Don't Smile and Laugh a Lot

Powertalkers don't smile often and they rarely smile broadly. The reason is obvious—smiles are very supportive responses to another speaker which give him or her more power. Generally speaking, powertalkers smile a shade less enthusiastically than other people. For instance, a powertalker will grin, with a slight curving of the lips over a closed mouth, while everyone else is smiling fully.

Subtalkers often operate in such a flutter of anxiety that they will smile broadly when no one else is, then completely forget to smile when everyone else has gone on to roaring laughter. They also use a distinctly subtalk smile called the "oblong" by G. L. Nierenberg and H. H. Calero in *How to Read a Person Like a Book*. The oblong is really a grimace that shows no real pleasure. The lips are drawn fully back from both sets of teeth forming an oblong with the lips. There's no depth or emotion in this smile and it's actually an expression of submissive anger used when subtalkers desperately want to escape from a situation . . . when they're forced to back down (especially in a humiliating manner) . . . or when they don't find the proceedings funny but don't want everyone else to know that.

Another subtalk smile is the "lip-in," which exposes the upper front teeth with the lower lip pulled into the teeth. This is a clear signal that the person using it feels subordinate to the person he or she is smiling at.

Subtalkers, of course, laugh a bit too much and often at inappropriate times. They also use a nervous laugh that's syncophantic and a sign of uncertainty. Nervous laughs aren't always obvious titters, but they can be recognized by looking at the body language. Nervous laughter is accompanied by many body movements that look more like discomfort than amusement (twisting and even entire shifts of the body). Needless to say, powertalkers suppress nervous laughs.

Using Your Body in Powertalk

There are several excellent books on body language; if you haven't read one, I suggest you do, since being able to read the body language of others in power struggle encounters can be an invaluable aid.

You'll find there are two basic styles of body language: the powertalker's assertive, assured, controlled, open style; and the subtalker's timid, hesitant, abruptly changing, closed style. Here's just a brief overview.

Powertalkers Expand into Space _____
The body language of a powertalker always indicates a willingness to occupy all available space and then some.

Whether sitting or walking, the powertalker stretches out. When moving, powertalkers walk freely, shoulders back, heads up, arms swinging. They have a long stride and move briskly, always looking as if they have a specific objective and a tight deadline.

When sitting, powertalkers are relaxed. Men spread their legs. Women avoid tightly constricted, prim positions. Both will spread their arms, taking the arms of a chair, stretching an arm along the back of the sofa, leaning arms across a desk.

Subtalkers, as you can guess, are the opposite. Their body language apologizes for taking up any space. They walk with head down to avoid casual eye contacts, shoulders hunched as if a whip were about to fall, stride shortened. They "sit tight," ready to spring into action if ordered, uneasy in the presence of power. The most obvious subtalkers sit on the end of the chair, leaning forward as if bowing.

Even when sitting, subtalkers keep arms and legs close to their bodies. When crossing legs, subtalkers will keep the crossed leg tight against the other—and they'll shift out of this position fairly soon, uncomfortable with the tension of trying to be relaxed and yet ready to go at the same time. Subtalkers change body position frequently, too, giving the impression of restlessness or nervousness. (A powertalker holds the same position longer than the average person, tends to signal restlessness by fiddling with something instead of moving the entire body.)

Powertalkers Invade Your Space

All creatures, including human beings, have a specific area of space around their bodies they feel belongs to them. If someone comes too close to you, you feel threatened because your personal space has been invaded (and the other person is now close enough to "get at you").

Powertalkers regularly threaten or invade the personal space of others in order to intimidate or enforce dominance. They threaten by making sudden, unexpected moves toward another. For example, you and a powertalker are relaxing in facing easy chairs and engaging in a mild power struggle. Without warning, the powertalker plants both feet on the floor, places hands on knees, and leans far forward toward you, thrusting his head out. This is a primitive ready-to-attack position of maximum power, and it is suddenly aimed directly at you, encroaching on the outer limits of your personal space. A Subtalker will respond to such a gesture by uncrossing legs, moving hands to a position on the arms of the chair (well away from the body, indicating he or she is not moving toward concealed weapons), sometimes with palms turned outward.

Powertalkers will also move right into your space, stretching an arm along a sofa behind you (it will make you feel very uneasy), sitting a little too close to you, spreading legs so that your legs touch (if you move your legs close together to get away, you make a submissive move), even touching you with pats or hugs.

Powertalkers Move Deliberately — Subtalkers Jerk

Powertalkers don't move often; when they do, they often move suddenly. But the movement is a complete movement to a different body position with a different message. For instance, in response to the spring-to-attack position discussed above, another powertalker might move his or her feet away from the body or apart, lean back even more, put elbows on chair arms, steeple fingers, and smile slightly. This series of moves becomes a total body message of complete confidence and indifference to the other's threat.

Subtalkers not only move around a lot (fidget) but make a lot of partial moves that have no real meaning except to communicate anxiety. They rarely hold relaxed positions long. Even when trying to be relaxed, they often look as though they're shrinking away from you rather than sitting back at ease.

A Few Key Points to Watch in Body Language

Body language can give you important messages during power encounters. For example:

1. Does the body language match what's being said and how it's being said? An opponent could be very aggressive verbally but submissive in body language. The body is usually telling the truth because we have less awareness and control over it.

2. Has the body language shifted from powertalk to subtalk? This is a clear alert that your opponent is ready to submit and you need only put on a little more pressure. This is also true if the body language starts shifting back and forth from power positions to submissive positions.

3. Is there a rigidity to the powertalk body languages that hints at a deliberate and uncomfortable effort to maintain the positions? If so, your opponent may be a new powertalker who is consciously trying to use powertalk body language but isn't comfortable with it yet. (You can test this by watching to see if he or she starts to slip into subtalk positions from time to time then suddenly reverses back to powertalk.) To gain the advantage with a new powertalker, raise the level of aggression of your power struggle substantially, or adopt a patronizing role of an experienced powertalker encouraging a beginner.

Summary

A large part of any powertalk is the nonverbal part of language which consists of your voice, facial expressions, and body language.

A powertalk voice utilizes the following elements:

Volume—slightly loud but not a shout.

Pitch—low-pitched voices have more authority.

Speed—slightly slower than the average for your area.

Breath—slightly breathy, never sharp; powertalkers never run out of breath in the middle of a sentence.

Rhythm—when spoken language has a definite rhythm, the voice is more impressive, and the content is more easily remembered.

If the people you want to be codominant with or dominant over look down on your accent, try to get rid of it. If your accent makes you more impressive with these people, retain it.

Enunciate clearly; subtalkers mumble because they're afraid to be heard.

Powertalkers maintain a lot of eye contact with others and use eye contact to intimidate, dominate, and deliver specific messages.

A powertalk face is a poker face with little change of expression. Powertalkers smile less often than other people and generally smile less broadly than others; they are especially stingy about smiling at what others say. Powertalkers also laugh less often and never use a nervous laugh.

Powertalk body language is confident, assured, and uses space (it's expansive whether sitting or walking). Powertalkers also invade the space of others, move less often than subtalkers, and make total moves to new body positions with new messages.

THE POWERTALK STYLE

Our personalities are complex, including everything from our sense of humor to our food preferences. We wouldn't want to revise our entire personality to become powertalkers, nor is there any need to. However, there are certain personal traits that we must develop to become effective powertalkers, which contribute to the degree that people are willing to perceive us as leaders.

The Seven Basics of the Powertalk Style

1. You Direct the Action

Dominant people act; submissive people react. The person who sets the direction—whether in a relationship, group, or organization—soon takes leadership. Even those who don't set directions for others but have very strong personal direction win respect. That's why the first rule of powertalk is to try to get credit for action by choosing, initiating, or implementing it.

Children and adolescents who want leadership figure out that if they create a quest for their peer group, they can mastermind it. Adults in corporate structures are quickly recognized as leaders if they initiate projects. Even in families with an old-fashioned structure where the man is the head of the house, women create personal power domains by asserting "ownership" of the home based on responsibility for domestic affairs.

Thinking up a project or activity works only as long as you can get it adopted by presenting it forcefully. Powertalk aims at starting and directing action, proposing solutions, and setting goals. Subtalkers, on the other hand, tend to surrender the idea they've come up with by being tentative. For example: "What do you think about going out to dinner tonight?"

A Powertalker makes definite statements: "Let's go out to dinner tonight." . . . "We need to take inventory right away." . . . "The pictures have to be hung before closing today." . . . "Nobody leaves the studio until this scene is reshot."

Powertalkers are equally forceful in responding to action suggested by others. A subtalker uses phrases that respond with support, supplements, or passive resistance, such as, "Terrific, what a great idea." . . . "Do we have to?" . . . "Whatever you say." . . . "What movie do you want to see?"

Powertalkers assume they know the best way to implement an idea so their response is a bid for taking control: "I'll start the clerks on inventory tomorrow evening; can you work late next Tuesday to review the figures with me?" . . . "Good idea, here's my floor plan for hanging the pictures."

One of my clients used this technique to make the switch from secretary to management. She'd been handling liaisons with a computer service bureau for several months when her boss announced that the company was establishing an in-house computer service department. She responded with a detailed outline of problems with the service bureau and specific recommendations to prevent similar difficulties in the new system. Because her reaction made her part of the implementation, she was invited to serve on the planning committee; by the time the department was operational, she was its manager.

2. You Issue the Commands _____

Powertalkers believe their instructions and orders are obeyed more readily and accurately so they don't hesitate to direct others. That doesn't mean powertalkers strut around like generals barking out terse instructions like, "You drive!" Good powertalkers avoid arousing unnecessary hostility. Requests and even statements of desires are still powertalk if they achieve the desired result. "Would you please drive?" or even "I'm too tired to drive" can elicit better cooperation from a spouse or fellow car pool member. In fact, powertalk commands are often less dictatorial than those issued by a subtalker since powertalkers assume obedience will automatically follow.

A powertalker understands the different types of command forms and uses the one that achieves results with the minimum degree of force. Here's how it works:

Arbitrary commands are snapped out like a Marine drill sargeant. Such harsh orders are appropriate only in situations where:

(a) there's a mutually understood possibility that a weaker command might not be obeyed . . .

(b) you're clearly in a position of sufficient authority to back up your threat and will do so (by fighting, suing, going to the authorities, or inflicting punishment) . . . and

(c) you're willing to accept the resulting hostility.

The only other time arbitrary commands are acceptable is when instant obedience could save lives. This is the rationale behind the military's use of harsh commands and applies equally to the person who yells: "Out of the water NOW!" without taking the time to politely explain that a great white shark is nearby.

Using arbitrary commands in a situation where you must be obeyed no matter how you issue the order is bullying. The boss who tells a subordinate: "Get the Johnson file NOW! Snap to it!" is inviting the subordinate to either quit or engage in long-term resistance and sabotage.

Directional commands are instructions issued without the frills of courtesy. Directional commands are used by people who are working together on a mutual project with mutual goals or by superiors to subordinates who work in close partnership and require instruction. Examples include the spouse who says, "Get me the hammer, honey." . . . the executive who tells a secretary, "Bring the Johnson files and then call Copco to confirm tomorrow's meeting." . . . and the team member who says, "You catch that one."

This command form is inappropriate in situations where obedience cannot be automatically assumed. For instance, if you tell your child's friend, "Put your glass in the sink," you may later hear the friend say, "Your Mom's kind of bossy, isn't she?" Telling a fellow executive, "Bring me your file on Johnson" may end up in a battle royal over your right to command.

Request commands are polite requests that don't assume obedience. Request commands may be courteous versions of instructional commands when given to people who must obey. For instance, asking your secretary, "Can you take a letter now?" assumes she will do so immediately—although the door is open for her to respond, "I'm doing this research you asked for; can it wait a half hour?"

Request commands are also used with people who don't have to obey you but probably will if you don't rile them.

Examples include asking your child's friend, "Would you please put your glass in the sink?" or requesting a co-worker, "Could you please bring me your file on Johnson as so soon as possible?"

Interactive commands imply a team effort in which you're participating. "Let's get this inventory done tonight," is an order when issued to a subordinate but seeks to generate willingness and cooperation by indicating you're part of the project, too.

Interactive commands can also be used to take over since you essentially become the director whenever you're the one who establishes the deadline or the goals. So an interactive command like, "Let's work on our batting practice now" is really a take-over bid.

Deferential commands are pure subtalk. An overpolite form of command that seeks to disguise the demand and/or apologize for it is never used in powertalk. For example, when a boss tells a secretary, "If it's not too much trouble, would you please bring the Johnson file? Thanks a lot," he or she is giving the secretary the right to say, "Sorry, it *is* too much trouble right now." The secretary might even ignore the boss and when he or she later asks what happened, respond, "Oh, I didn't realize I had to do it."

Whenever you feel people don't do what you tell them to, examine the command form you're using. Deferentials are frequently the culprit.

3. You Are Precise About What You Want _

You sound sure when your language is precise. That's why powertalk always uses the most exact words possible—particularly the proper terms for things. "I'll see you at ten o'clock sharp" is powertalk; "I'll see you around ten-ish" is subtalk.

Precision gives your speech the credibility and authority that's a crucial part of powertalk. So whenever possible, extend this precision to the point of being technical and mathematical. If you don't know the right terms, make your generic descriptions as exact as possible. If, for example, you don't know the word "bevel," say, "Cut the edge to a 45-degree angle." Never say, "Sort of shave it under like this," while hacking with your hand.

Precision is a way of being sure your commands will be obeyed correctly; use of it in noncommand situations is a signal that you're used to commanding others.

4. You're Concise

The shorter the sentence, the stronger it is! Dominant people pare their words to the bone, say what they have to say clearly, and then stop. There are a number of reasons for this:

- Lengthening a statement, no matter how you do it, softens the statement's impact nine times out of ten. Subtalkers intentionally lengthen their statements to render them less controversial. For example:
  POWERTALK: "I don't agree."
  SUBTALK: "Well, it's only my opinion, of course, and some of you might not agree with me, but I really don't think that's such a terrific idea, although perhaps there are some other reasons behind it that I don't understand."

- There's no way to lengthen a statement neutrally. A short statement is usually unequivocal and somewhat threatening. Longer statements require more words and modified grammar, which change the meaning. Even one word can weaken implicit threats. For example:
  POWERTALK: "Don't do that."
  SUBTALK: "Please don't do that." Or longer and weaker, "I really wish you wouldn't do that."

There is an exception, however—statements lengthened with threats are even stronger. For example: "Don't do that *or you'll be sorry*" or "I *happen to know for a fact* that it's dangerous to do that."

- People pay more attention to short statements, too. Subtalkers often try to dominate conversations by extending their statements to keep the floor, but invariably they lose the attention of their audience. For proof, guess which of the following is powertalk:
  (a) "We have a serious deficit here. Look at page four of the financial report."
  (b) "I want to call your attention to several different matters here, some of which are more important than others, but there's one paramount problem I think we all ought to focus on as quickly as possible. It's quite serious and I've got a number of solutions that you might want to consider. Now, if you'll turn to—let me see, oh yes, here it is— page four in the current financial report, which my staff worked very hard on getting ready for this meeting. Here on page four, starting about halfway down the page, you'll see some totals at the end of the financial summary for the operating year 1982. Notice the final figure. It's a deficit. And, as I said, that's pretty important. In fact, I'd say it's the most serious thing we have to discuss today."

- Do I have to point out that (b) is subtalk? Did you even finish it or did you quickly realize that a subtalker's endless monologue is dulling and self-defeating?

5. You're Polite but Never Obsequious _____

The fifth element of the powertalk style is courtesy. Powertalkers are never so excessively polite that they seem to apologize for their existence, seem grateful for attention, or are otherwise uncomfortable in their surroundings. Too much courtesy is a subtalk signal of anxiety and the need to please. Rudeness is also subtalk, indicating you're too ignorant or insecure to treat others respectfully.

The ideal courtesy for a powertalker is "noblesse oblige," an effortless courtesy that shows you have perfect command of yourself and the situation. It's courtesy as graciousness, with no sense of approval-seeking, self-apology, awe, or sarcasm.

Powertalk courtesy is always appropriate to the situation, too. Even a simple "please" can be out of place when you're constantly making requests (working on a cooperative project, for instance). Not only do the courtesy words add unnecessary verbiage at such times, they also lose any impact and are perceived as being automatic, without any real feeling. A warm "thank you" at the end of the project or after a busy day will gain far more mileage.

Some powertalkers are able to gain a great deal of status by using absolutely perfect etiquette. If you can pull this off with authority, you can leave everyone else feeling distinctly lowborn. However, be careful where you play this game. If everyone else is casual yet accomplished and assured, you could end up looking as ridiculous as Margaret Dumont surrounded by the Marx Brothers.

One of the most important parts of powertalk courtesy is that you must never apologize for yourself. Acknowledge your mistakes and their effects on others, by all means, but don't apologize for your character flaws, any weaknesses, or anxiety. Self-apologies are a form of submission since they admit you're worried that others might be displeased with you, and they offer the opportunity for others to express displeasure punitively.

A POWERTALK APOLOGY:

"I'm sorry I didn't call you sooner. I know it must have inconvenienced you. Unfortunately, I couldn't get to a phone." (That covers it: You were in error, it was unintentional and not a sign of disrespect. And you recognize it caused a problem.)

A SUBTALK APOLOGY:

"I'm so terribly sorry. I was running so late and I looked but just couldn't find a telephone. You weren't too inconvenienced, were you? I feel just terrible about it." (This apology gives people the upper hand and invites responses like, "I certainly hope you're sorry, do you realize you made me miss the supermarket and we had to have cold noodles for dinner. Why can't you be more responsible?")

It stands to reason that powertalkers also don't make promises they can't be sure they'll keep—or else they're setting up the need for another apology. Such promises, especially when added to an apology ("I'll never do it again") sound and feel like a small child humbly submitting to an angry adult—not a portrait of a good powertalker. People with power have no need to make promises to powerless people, so when you do make a promise, it should be offered with the attitude of bestowing a gracious favor.

The only time a promise can be effective is when you're powertalking up—speaking powertalk to someone with authority over you. When this happens and you believe you can keep the promise, apologize in a strong, dignified manner by simply making a statement like, "This won't happen again." If you have no control over keeping the promise, don't make it, no matter what the situation. Offer a simple reason, such as, "Sorry, but when I'm on the road, I can't always get to a phone on schedule."

Offering to make amends is pure subtalk at all times. Any offer to "make up for" your error is humbling yourself before another.

6. You Don't Brag but You Don't Wait to Be Discovered

There's scant room for humility in powertalk. If you're reticent, people may just assume you're a nobody and pass you by. If you humbly hang your head and murmer you're really not a very good tennis player, most people will not pursue the matter until they discover you won at Wimbledon two years ago.

Contrary to what your mother taught you, modesty doesn't work. No one is going to lift the bushel basket to find your light. And because your accomplishments and superior qualities bring you power and respect, it's important to tell others about these power bases to show that your powertalk is not all bluff.

However, on the other hand, if you're too forward and outspoken, you'll look so boastful that people will resent you and try to knock you down. Excessive claims of competence can also have a reverse impact—people suspect you can't possibly be as good as you say you are.

The best way to tell others how special you are is to "leak" information—dropping clues or teasers so others pursue you for further data. Then, under prodding, you can modestly reveal the facts about how wonderful you are. Leaking can be done by using nonverbal clues (props) or by dropping tantalizing hints during conversation. The ideal is a combination of both. Clues can be your clothes, accessories, your car, a beeper on your belt, a stethoscope snaking out of your back pocket, even a shrunken head over the fireplace. You can use almost anything to get people asking questions.

Nonverbal clues should be fairly obvious and used in places where the appropriate people will see them. For instance, business consultants can range from being extremely successful professionals who make more money consulting than they could with a full-time job to the long-term unemployed who are trying to supplement welfare checks. A fancy car and a home filled with antiques and original works of art won't tell a new business prospect that you're a successful consultant. However, if you wear a Saville Row suit, Sulka tie, Rolex watch, emerald ring, and carry a Mark Cross briefcase, the message is very clear.

The other way to leak information is to drop verbal

clues that are so intriguing that people are almost forced
to follow up by asking you to explain. For instance, suppose you've just testified before a congressional committe
about your work on alcoholism-treatment strategies and
you meet someone at a party. You can use a variety of
ploys to get your acquaintance to ask about your expertise: You can yawn a few times and when your acquaintance asks if you're tired, reply, "God, yes, these
Washington commutes are catching up with me. It was
fun the first couple of times I was called down, but now it's
just becoming hard work—underpaid work at that."

With such a lead, your acquaintance is bound to ask
questions that will let you explain how you're helping the
appropriations committee decide how to spend millions of
dollars.

Another way is to stare at your drink and say, "I'm
getting so I feel guilty every time I have a drink. Tip
O'Neill—the Speaker of the House, you know—told me I
was taking all the fun out of martinis for him, too."

You can also lead the conversation to topics that will let
you reveal your information naturally. For instance, you
could start asking your new friend about vacations, which
would lead to talking about air flights, which would let
you say, "Well, I don't know when I'm going to take my
next vacation, but it sure won't be on a plane. I've spent
enough time on planes lately to last ten years."

When setting up a conversation so you can drop your
bombshells of accomplishment, be careful to listen to the
other person's responses. If he or she answers with extreme simplicity, immediately following up with your
great victory can seem like a putdown. If you opened the
topic of vacations, for example, and the other person said,
"I usually take a packaged bus tour. Someday I'd like to
take a plane, though," you certainly wouldn't want to
brag that you've logged more time than an Air Force general.

Another way to direct the conversation is to turn your

clues into humorous anecdotes. Perhaps a business acquaintance inquires about your boss, for example. "Oh,
she's furious with me!" you answer, with a chuckle.
"We've been so busy I completely forgot to tell her I'm in
the current edition of *Who's Who* and she found out by
overhearing my secretary talking to the receptionist. She
can't believe I would forget such a thing and is sure I had
some nefarious purpose in keeping it from her!"

7. Never Put Yourself Down

It goes without saying that if you shouldn't be humble
and modest about your accomplishments, you certainly
shouldn't put yourself down. But putting yourself down is
such a major error that it deserves a separate explana-
tion.

NEVER SAY: "I'm not very smart."
            "Of course, I'm very young."
            "Naturally, you know much more about
            that than I do."
            "I know someone wonderful like you
            would never be interested in a poor slob
            like me."
            "I can't do that; I don't have the experi-
            ence."
            "Of course, I'm not beautiful."

When self-esteem is low, people form the habit of putting themselves down in front of others. Basically, self-
doubts make such people afraid to assert themselves as
worthwhile, attractive, accomplished, or competent.
They're afraid that if they do, they'll fail, be challenged,
or even attract laughter. And they try to lessen anxiety
by announcing their shortcomings first, hoping the other
person will deny them. This is very common, and most of
us do it occasionally.

But it's such self-destructive subtalk, you should make

a conscious effort to avoid it at all times. People often do come up with the compliments they're being manipulated into (although just as often they don't, leaving the "inviter" in a humiliating position), but the strategy is always self-defeating. Whether or not people deny your putdowns, they hear them and to a degree accept them. So any time you tell someone you're dumb or clumsy, they accept that this is at least partly true. And by calling attention to these flaws, you give them importance.

Remember that the first part of a powertalk encounter is comparison of one another's power strengths. Putting yourself down in situations like this is handing ammunition to the opposition. In addition, putting yourself down in order to invite positive reaction puts others in a position to accept or contradict—the dominant position. Putdowns are the worst forms of subtalk you can use!

Powertalk Is Confident, Positive, to the Point and Forceful

These seven basic elements alone can transform how others see you. They add up to speech that presents you as confident, capable, self-assured and forceful—the trademarks of leaders in all walks of life. But this is only the first step. As you go on, you'll find that it's just as easy to portray yourself as organized, intelligent, and levelheaded.

Summary

The seven basics of the powertalk style are:

1. You direct the action by thinking up projects and things to do. Present them positively and confidently and respond to the ideas of others in a way that lets you take control of the activity or focus it.

2. You issue commands with ease, selecting the appropriate command form for the situation (the right form is the one that people heed but don't resent).

3. You're precise—you use exact words, never vague generalities.

4. You're concise. The shorter the statement, the clearer it is and the stronger your position.

5. You're polite, using a gracious courtesy that never apologizes for yourself or seeks approval. You don't make promises you can't keep and you never offer to make amends when apologizing for a mistake.

6. You don't brag but you do let others know about your accomplishments. You use leaks—either nonverbal clues in the form of props or verbal hints that are too tantalizing to ignore.

7. You *never* put yourself down. This is the worst form of subtalk, inviting others to take power over you and advertising shortcomings that may not even be important until you mention them.

POWERTALKERS
USE THE SOUND
OF REASON

7

The last major element in speaking powertalk is learning to use the sound of reason. Messengers, elevator operators, and others who have little to think about at work can afford to be as muddle-headed as they like, but powerful people have responsibilities. They must analyze and solve problems logically, create plans that others can follow, establish goals, evaluate performances, measure results, and direct the efforts of subordinates.

Powertalk is filled with this sound of reason—a style and vocabulary that includes analytic, goal-directed, and evaluative functions. People who use reason sound like they know what they're doing and are used to leadership. The sound of reason makes the thought process seem to have greater clarity, depth, and breadth.

I used to know a creative director in advertising who used the sound of reason to astonishingly good effect. The man's ideas were really not that special—in fact, for a creative director he lacked imagination to a surprising degree. But the reasons why he did things the way he did were really remarkable. He would create a fairly pedestrian campaign for a product, and then, when challenged with more imaginative proposals, would defend himself with an overwhelming set of arguments containing statistics about the market for his product and long trains of logical deductions from premises which at least sounded unassailable.

Most creative people, being more intuitive than logical, were unable to stand up to him with arguments based on taste. And certain types of advertisers found his approach very reassuring, and were much more comfortable with it than with a more intuitive one.

If this man was able to get as far as he did supporting his rather mediocre ideas with the sound of reason, just imagine how far a really creative person could get.

The Seven
Elements of Reason

1. Formal Structure Makes Your Statements Sound More Important _____

People discuss serious matters in a structured presentation, rather than casual conversation. So when you shift to formality, you raise the level of discussion and your opinions and arguments sound more significant. For example:

> **SUBTALK** (Casual): *"Just because Consolidated is located near your office is no reason to give them the contract. We can do better than them in a lot of ways."*

> **POWERTALK** (Structured): *"Consolidated's proximity to your office is an inadequate rea-*

son for giving them the contract. We're able to outperform them in three ways: First, we're more experienced in the field. Second, we have a reputation for reliable, prompt performance which they do not. And third, we can underbid them. Furthermore, the only advantage to their proximity is that it cuts their travel overhead. Unless they're willing to pass the savings to you, this gives you no advantage whatsoever. We're willing to absorb our transportation costs out of our profit margin at no cost to you. Therefore, there's no reason why we should not be the contractor of choice."

2. Logic Builds an Unassailable Argument ____

There's another important difference between the examples above. The subtalk statement sounds like a plaintive complaint that's little more than one person's opinion. The powertalk statement proceeds step by step, creating an airtight case through the use of logic. The argument sounds so authoritative and comprehensive that it's hard to find any way to object to it. That's what logic does and that's exactly what a powertalker wants.

Logic is a way of reasoning from a set of premises; so that if the premises are true, the conclusions are true. Logic is *not* a guarantee of truth—it's possible to reach a set of false conclusions from true premises. It's also possible to reach true conclusions from false premises which, though they appear to be true, contain a hidden fault; when that happens, the conclusions usually came first through intuition or observation and the logic was "tacked on" to establish credibility.

Correct logic is a powerful tool for powertalk. (Even incorrect logic can convince those who have no training in it—because it sounds so reasonable and well thought out.)

If you have any doubts about your ability to understand logic, I recommend you study it. It's easy and fun, and most rhetoric books will teach you the fundamentals of logical thinking and writing.

Because logic is so important in powertalk, the vocabulary of logic can have an impact even when you're not using the reasoning of logic. You can give an air of authority and credibility to your speech by adopting words and phrases like "premises," "given," "it follows that," "therefore," "in conclusion," "corollary to that" and "Q.E.D." You can also strengthen the impact if you present your basic material in outline form and enumerate the points of your argument.

3. The Analytical Approach Makes You Sound Like a Very Clear Thinker

Powertalkers can give the impression of brilliance by presenting their thoughts analytically. By summarizing all the key points and identifying and weighing all possible alternatives, they leave little room for other people's ideas.

For example: "We have several ways of competing here. First, we can bring in a cheaper product, cut our profit margin, and make our money on mass sales. Second, we can put our efforts into packaging and advertising and develop a superior brand image which will enable us to outsell our competitors without cutting prices. Or third, we can produce a higher-quality product in smaller quantities, become known as the best, and then set our prices at a level which will enable us to make a healthy profit."

4. You Gain Control of Action by Staying Solution-Oriented

A top corporate executive with a reputation for identifying new executive talent once told me his technique was simple: "The person who will always be a follower brings me messages. 'John Smith called and wants to talk to you about a problem he has,' this person will say. The ones with real potential offer me solutions. They'll say, 'John Smith called with a problem and it seems to me you have the following three solutions.' Right away, I know they're thinking, they're pushing for more responsibility, and they're trying to gain some power."

Powertalkers *never* talk about problems or needs without recommendations for specific action, because acceptance of the solution is the real acknowledgment of power. By presenting situations analytically and logically, powertalkers make their recommendations sound like the only rational solutions. Such a presentation is difficult to attack and usually requires a strong personal stand. Subtalkers are locked out; they may carp at details to try to preserve some power, but they're too afraid to offer real countersolutions.

A powertalk example: "At present, we don't have the production facilities for large-scale, low-cost production nor do we have the capital for either increased production or a major advertising effort. That leaves the third option, producing a premium product, as the only viable goal at present."

To attack this presentation, another powertalker would say, "Now wait a minute. I don't agree that you've explored all options. I see a fourth solution . . ."

In other words, the attacker must stop the logical, analytical flow and backtrack. This puts the attacker on the line personally, since the initial powertalker can respond, "Oh, I considered that but it was so impractical, it wasn't worth discussing here," which in effect, accuses the attacker of being a muddy thinker or someone who can't tell trivia from substance.

5. Consolidate Control Through Implementation

Once a powertalker has presented the reasons why his or her solution is the best, he or she immediately starts implementation, retaining control of the action and shutting out any objections to the proposed solution.

For example: "Okay, if we're going to stress a premium product, we'll need to upgrade our materials. John, can you get some samples for us to review? We'll also need to improve workmanship. Mary, will you go over the job descriptions and prepare revisions? Let's start to get our information together and discuss it further next Thursday afternoon. Is that all right with everyone? Fine, we'll meet then."

Once again, to counter this approach requires a great deal of courage, and willingness to deal with put-downs, scorn, and other powertalking tactics. The powertalker has established momentum with the sound of reason and is fully in control. An opponent must take a very strong stand to break into this smooth flow. For instance: "I don't think we're ready to start implementing this yet. I have some strong objections to making such drastic changes in our systems."

The powertalker could well make such an interruption sound like the statement of a spoiler or fault-finder who has nothing positive and useful to offer. For instance: "Oh, really! I do hope you have solutions to offer and not just objections. This company is in trouble and we're not in a position where we can afford the luxury of fault-finding. We need a solution now."

6. Calm and Rational Argument Is Usually the Powertalk Approach

The responsibilities of power often necessitate standing up for your opinions. Not surprisingly, argument is an important element of powertalk. But there are different ways of arguing. Generally, powertalkers use logical argument, presenting their positions with analytical techniques, and remain emotionally cool.

In most cases, emotional argument is subtalk. (Emotional argument relies for its effectiveness on yelling, tears, threats, persistence, pleading, guilt manipulation, and the like.) But there are times when powertalkers can't avoid emotional argument or use it quite deliberately, even pretending to be emotional when they're not. There are three common situations in which emotional argument is a part of powertalk.

1. When there are close personal bonds between adversaries (family members, close friends, and lovers, for instance), emotional argument is often unavoidable and may well be the best tactic (anyone who has ever been completely cowed by a crying, martyred, persistent parent or partner can attest to this).

2. In power arenas where great masses of people must be swayed, emotion can create an irrational swell of mood that carries along even those who know better. Hitler was a master at this. Politicians, union officials, and other leaders who deal with large groups skillfully use emotional argument when dealing with their constituencies and then switch to rational argument in communicating with their peers. Lawyers often use emotion with juries, logic with judges.

3. On rare occasions, powertalking business people will use emotional argument (and even tantrums) to win a victory they're not entitled to on the evidence. Employers sometimes manipulate employees into working overtime without pay by moaning about how bad business is or implying that the employee is in danger of losing the job. An explosive loss of temper can sometimes help a powertalker gain control of a meeting, get a bill reduced, obtain delivery faster. Powertalkers who use this tactic do so very rarely, however, since a consistent display of emotion can build a reputation for instability and erode a power base. These displays are also usually com-

pletely false—an act put on to achieve a specific objective.

It's even possible for extremely skillful infighters to combine the elements of logic and emotion into one argument, generating psychological effects that are hard to combat. For instance, a father might be very determined that his son enter medical school to sustain a family tradition. All sorts of emotional pressures might be used: The father has a heart problem and is getting upset. . . . As a doctor himself, he's already spoken to the medical school, and put his own reputation on the line. . . . The mother cautions the son to be a good boy. As emotionally compelling as these ploys are, the son may resist them as not being adequate enough reasons to change his entire life. (He may be deeply moved but resists, in part, because the arguments are emotional rather than rational.) Then a spurious but logically credible economic analysis of the financial rewards of a medical career is added, seemingly providing that medical school is the best of all possible choices for the boy. While actually giving in to the emotional pressures, the boy seizes on the logical argument to justify the "right" decision.

7. Documentation Can Prove You're Right Even When You're Not!

Evidence counts as much in powertalk as it does in a courtroom! The more good evidence you can cite, the more convincing you are, and the harder it is to attack you. Evidence proves that what you're saying is not a personal opinion but an accepted, valid point of view with a power of its own. And this power of evidence extends to you, reinforcing your own validity as an authority.

Why is evidence so convincing? First of all, few people will know enough about any particular area to question even a little bit of evidence. Although the world is full of people who will happily argue matters of opinion with you ad infinitum, very few will bother to take ten minutes in the library to check on the facts. Furthermore, most people are so busy covering up, that they don't dare challenge anyone who could reveal their ignorance. So when you start citing evidence as part of your presentation, a lot of people who would stand up to your aggression, objective style, and logic, will back off and let you win.

Skilled powertalkers always support their arguments with evidence. Even when challenged on these facts, it's often your word against the other person's, or your source of facts against theirs—so nothing is lost.

Obviously, if your evidence is totally invented and you're called on it, you'll be at a serious disadvantage. But this rarely happens; even when it does, the proof comes so long after the original discussion that the spectators have gone home. (At worst, you can always find some way of claiming that wasn't quite what you said in the first place or you were misled by inaccurate data.)

Making up evidence is seldom necessary, however, since "facts" are easy to find. In most cases, you can quickly locate the right facts to support anything. If necessary, you can always take statements out of context.

Just one note of warning: Never try to support an argument with a technical specialist by spouting statistics about his or her field. Not only will the specialist know the deficiencies of the evidence (and most evidence has flaws), but he or she can probably delight in citing counterdocumentation. In specialist confrontations, your best strategy is to claim you see the overall picture better. Prove this by citing statistics or data from an area that interfaces or overlaps the specialty.

For example: Suppose you are discussing your plans for a new magazine for nurses with a nursing specialist who can help finance your project. To convince the specialist, do you tell her how many nurses there are, what their major problems are, or how much nurses will pay for a professional publication?

If you foolishly make such remarks, you open the door for the specialist to snap, "Where did you get that stuff?" and contradict all your facts with data that is more authoritative, recent, or more complete.

Unless you're absolutely sure your data is accurate or wish to show you've done your "homework" and offer facts as a preface, you should focus on other areas that are new to the specialist. For instance: "The actual number of nurses in the country isn't nearly as important as the availability of mailing lists that contain nurses grouped by specialty and years of experience. Now I've done an analysis of the lists that give us our prime market and I've got their performance history here . . ."

While marshaling evidence, however, don't forget that powertalk is concise. You don't need to overwhelm opponents by presenting every available fact. This is what subtalkers do as they bury the key facts in a sea of irrelevant and boring details. Their listeners lose track of what's going on, decide the subtalker is incapable of determining significance, and dismiss the entire argument. Make your points quickly, provide three or four of the best pieces of evidence you can find, and then move on!

Practice the Sound of Reason Until It's Your Natural Style of Expression

The sound of reason is one of the most important parts of powertalk. The moment you begin to use it, you'll notice that people react to you in a different way, paying attention to what you have to say, believing you, following your direction and suggestions. That's why it's important to consciously develop your skills in this area. You'll find it helpful in the beginning to outline your presentations to establish a logical, step-by-step, analytical approach that smoothly leads to your conclusions. Plan your use of documentation. Think about how you will deal with people who might try to interrupt you.

Try to use the sound of reason constantly for a while. Within a short time, you'll notice that you automatically start presenting new ideas and opinions in this way. And at that point, you'll have taken an important step toward becoming a powertalk master.

Summary

The sound of reason is a speaking style used by top corporate leaders in all areas to persuade others to accept opinions, courses of action, and ideas. People who use the sound of reason are perceived as clear thinkers, highly intelligent and forceful.

There are seven components to the sound of reason:

1. Formal structure, which uses precise terms, correct grammar, and a slightly pedantic tone, lends authority and importance to your statements.

2. Logic is a way of reasoning from a set of premises so that, if the premises are true, the conclusions are true. Logic leads other people to think the way you want; by agreeing with your facts, they are inclined to agree with your conclusions. The language of logic can have a positive impact on listeners even when you're not using the principles of logic.

3. An analytical approach makes you look as if you have considered all the facts and their implications.

4. When you offer solutions, you gain power. Logic, analysis, and formality are the tools for presenting your solutions and laying the groundwork for their acceptance.

5. Setting goals insures that your solutions are accepted and that you retain control of implementa-

tion. Move smoothly from a presentation of a solution to establishing the goals for implementation. Take victory away from others' solutions by establishing goals for them.

6. Powertalkers normally use a calm, rational approach in an argument. Their arguments are logical and very cool emotionally. Emotional argument is subtalk except when close personal relationships are involved: when you wish to sway masses of people, or when you wish to win in a situation where the facts are against you. Do not use emotional argument in formal or business situations except on very rare occasions.

7. Documentation or evidence to support your ideas and opinions can help win over others since most people are too lazy to search out the truth of your documentation. Totally false evidence is seldom necessary as it's so easy to find facts to support your stand, no matter what it is. Be careful not to put your audience to sleep with an endless array of facts (that's the insecurity of subtalk). Choose a few pieces of evidence to prove you're not alone in holding such an opinion and then move on.

Practice using the sound of reason by outlining your presentation in writing. It won't take long for this approach to become automatic.

TAKING POWER

8

The individual who speaks powertalk is attempting to assume more power in his or her life. But just speaking powertalk will not be enough; you have to want power and be willing to fight for it. Few people are just going to roll over and let you take their power, and those who will allow it usually don't have any in the first place.

Whenever you encounter a new person, you are going to go through a process that will determine the structure of your relationship. By opting to become a powertalker, you have assumed a basic goal in all your relationships, which is to be accepted by that person as at least a codominant. That is, a someone who is their equal and who must be treated with deference and respect. Furthermore, there are some circumstances when your goal will be much more ambitious than this; it will be to be dominant, and to force the other person to submit to your will. (We will talk about when and how to do this later.)

To become a codominant or dominant person, you are going to have to do more than speak powertalk. You are going to have to start fighting for dominance in those areas where you used to submit. Although the techniques of powertalk will tell you how to fight, they are useless without having the determination to fight. As long as you can maintain your decision to be powerful and not to submit in a power struggle, you will always be at least a codominant. It is only after you lose heart, give up and start subtalking, that you become powerless.

The first point you have to think about is that everyone involved in a power struggle is going through a process similar to yours. That is, they will be sizing you up, comparing you with themselves. Then, on the basis of this comparison, they will be trying to decide whether you are a codominant, someone they can dominate, or someone to whom they will have to submit. Some of the people you will be coming up against already hold a lot of power in their lives, and are used to others relating to them submissively. They will not grant you power easily.

On the other hand, you will soon have some distinct advantages over them:

- You will be aware of all the implicit and psychological levels of the power struggle, while chances are they are only functioning on an intuitive level.

- You will have decided even before entering the struggle to demand to be at least codominant (highway patrolmen and muggers excepted), while they will be setting their goals for the relationship on the basis of how they compare themselves to you. Thus, you are less likely to follow the impulse to submit than they are.

- You will have at your disposal everything that is contained in this book: knowledge of the psychodynamics of the power struggle, awareness of powertalk, and familiarity with the strategic use of powertalk in a great variety of situations.

To begin, study the stages of the powertalk struggle in the following pages. They are the framework within which all powertalk encounters take place. Furthermore, try to connect what you read with your own experience . . . because you are reading not only to learn, but to change your psychological attitudes.

The Struggle

All powertalk struggles—even those between friends and lovers—have a serious, sometimes even brutal, undertone. In the cowboy movies, the guy in the black hat kicks the barroom door open and blasts anyone who doesn't kiss his boots. Then, after everyone is sufficiently humiliated, the guy in the white hat walks in, shoots the guns out of his hands, and gives him twenty-four hours to get out of town.

Modern power struggles have some of the same tension as in the above cowboy scene, but they are usually much more civilized, and we have many more alternatives before we are reduced to physical combat. Here are the three basic stages that civilized power struggles go through:

1. Sizing up _____

This exploratory phase takes place during the introductions, greetings, and preliminary small talk of conversation. In fact, the main purpose of this small talk is to evaluate the person you're meeting, and make a decision about whether to engage in a struggle or to capitulate.

Your inner mind makes dozens of observations and conclusions during this brief period, covering such topics as:

- What you already know: whether this person is powerful in terms of knowledge, education, career, financial standing, status, class, or some other qualification that commands your respect. Even before you come face to face with a celebrity or person with a reputation of great power, you may have decided the other person merits your deference. However, you may still engage in a power struggle in order to get yourself accepted as a power person in your own right, particularly if the other person treats you as beneath contempt.

- What you see: Does this person appear better dressed, wealthier-looking, more successful than you? Has he or she arrived with powerful friends who seem to be close buddies? Is he or she wearing or carrying something that tells you about deference-commanding qualifications (such as a Phi Beta Kappa key, or a beeper)? What you're looking for at this point is evidence of a person's power base—the qualifications the person has to command real respect.

In addition to looking for symbols of real power, you should assess the other person's powertalk capability at this point:

- What's happening: Does the way this person is talking indicate he or she is used to being in command and expects others to knuckle under and even offer worship? Is this person being extremely friendly or cool?

- What you're concluding: Does this person seem to be the type who will fight for dominance to the bitter end or can you expect a complete cave-in if you just push a little? What sort of relationship do you want with this person, and does he or she seem to agree?

Within a few moments, you will make your preliminary decisions. You may think this person is smarter, richer, and more powerful than you, and you'll submit accordingly. Or you may not be willing to shoot it out with this very aggressive person who seems intent on getting your submission so you let him be boss. If you decide to submit, no matter what you've determined earlier about taking a more powerful role, you'll switch automatically to subtalk and you will not be accorded the rights and respect of a power person. You may be treated with kindness (you no longer have the option of demanding it), but it will be a patronizing sort of treatment that holds no real respect for your abilities or virtues.

However, if you decide that you compare pretty well with this person, you move to the next power struggle stage. You should make this decision most of the time.

2. Sparring

If your preliminary conclusion is to insist on fair treatment, you and your powertalk opponent next test the accuracy of your observations, as well as one another's willingness to fight, by using sporadic, tentative powertalk feints that present you as a powerful person and test your opponent's strength. During sparring, you push to get the conversation centered on topics that display your authority or expertise and drop hints about your power base. You also engage in light powertalk—interrupting, for instance, changing the topic of conversation, insisting on your opinion, imposing your judgment. However, you do all this with delicacy, leaving the door open to retreat by pretending you weren't really powertalking or got carried away.

Sparring may result in revelations that cause you to back off. Perhaps you learn that your opponent owns the company you work for and wisdom tells you simply to accept the role the owner wants you to take, at least for the moment. Or you may conclude that you most definitely want to change the power roles. If you decide this, you enter into a true power struggle until an outcome is reached, in which you must aim for dominance. Even when you only want to be codominant friends (or lovers) on an equal footing, you cannot avoid the "fight" element of the struggle—you have to aim to win. However, you can avoid demolishing the other by using less hostile and hurtful tactics that don't destroy the relationship. This works provided the other person has the same goal in mind. If your spouse wants either dominance or a divorce, you cannot hope to win a power struggle in which you want to realign the power balance to a relationship of codominants. In a situation like this, you would pull your punches and your spouse would not; it would be like fighting with marshmallows against poisoned arrows.

That's why sparring determines not only whether or not your initial observations about the other person's power base were correct, but whether or not you have an agreement on what sort of struggle you're going to engage in—in other words, your ultimate goals and how ruthless the struggle will be. Remember, however, that even when there's an unspoken agreement to avoid going for the jugular, you must enter the struggle determined to win!

3. Combat

The power struggle now moves into the aggressive phase, which escalates in intensity through three levels, until someone submits:

- **Polite combat.** Although your efforts to assert dominance become more open, and your conversation becomes argumentative, polite combat remains within the rules set by society for acceptable behavior between people who are not enemies. At this level, your friendly smile may occasionally be a bit forced but you remain fairly cool and casual.

- **Open combat.** The people standing near you are now aware that a struggle is taking place. You and your opponent mutually acknowledge one another as adversaries and you threaten one another that you're willing to do anything that's socially acceptable to gain control (although this could be a bluff). Despite the fact that conversation is hostile and you may bring bystanders and friends into the confrontation as allies, you both continue to operate within the rules of society. You could end up in a fist fight if that's an acceptable alternative in your circle, but it will be a fair fight.

- **Mortal combat.** In this final stage, anything goes. You are committed to not surrendering and are willing to intimidate, demoralize, and destroy your enemy by any means at your disposal. If that means destroying your enemy's allies, too bad. The rules of society are set aside and warfare is total.

Few power struggles end in mortal combat, or even open combat, and one of the purposes of powertalk is to win without reaching these stages. However an *apparent* willingness to let a power struggle escalate into the final stages can be a critical element in winning difficult encounters. However, it is dangerous; it can either get you into a physical fight you don't want, or lead to your being socially ostracized.

Most powertalk struggles are not personal but goal directed. Their aims are things like leadership of a group, getting your project accepted, or establishing new rules for a relationship. Powertalk that threatens people is counterproductive because it destroys relationships and creates enemies. Most powerful people understand this, and will follow a blistering attack by patting you on the shoulder and saying, "Nothing personal, of course."

Power Struggles Don't Always Need to End in Victory or Loss

Power struggles can have a variety of outcomes which can occur at any point during the struggle.

Submission. One solution, obviously, is submission. Either you or your opponent reaches a maximum limit of aggressiveness and then backs off, acknowledging the other as dominant (or permitting the other to establish the relationship). Unless the struggle is renewed later, this relationship will prevail.

One of the finer points of powertalk is to create situations in which the only response to your action or statement is at a level of aggressiveness that the other person is unwilling to take. For instance, you may say or do something that assumes your superiority and dominance over the other person. To counter your powertalk ploy, the other person must act so aggressively that he or she can't take the step. If you're a more skillful powertalker than the other person, you may simply leave the other person without any response except to submit. (I'll show you how to do this and how to counter such ploys in full detail later on.)

Truce. Another outcome is a truce, a peer relationship where you and your opponent acknowledge each other as codominants. Neighbors in a middle-class suburb are frequently peers in a permanent truce. Co-workers may establish temporary codominant relationships with an unspoken agreement to resume the power struggle at some point in the future (near promotion time, perhaps). Powertalking peers speak a special language to one another that retains the elements of powertalk but carefully avoids any challenge or aggression. (I'll explain this peertalk in more detail later.)

Retreat. Opponents can also separate at any point during the power struggle. The separation may be permanent, in which case the two people go out of their way to avoid each other. Or the separation may be temporary, a respite during which both recoup their strength, plot out their strategies, and then start struggling anew. Retreats are very effective ways of turning the tables when the struggle is going against you.

Even when the outcome is definitely decided with a clear winner, victory is not necessarily final. The power struggle can resume whenever there's a change in the status of one of the participants. When a child grows up, the submissive woman discovers the women's movement, one person has therapy or gets a better job, or someone reads this book, he or she may decide the power balance needs adjustment, and reopen the struggle. You can never be absolutely secure in your power, and you never need to feel locked into being powerless.

Summary

The first step in becoming a powertalker is to decide firmly to be accepted as a dominant, powerful person. In most cases, this will be challenged at least initially, and you'll have to engage in a power struggle.

Power struggles consist of three stages: sizing up, during which you compare yourself to your opponent and decide whether or not to challenge; sparring, during which you make tentative feints with powertalk to confirm your decision to challenge; and combat, which escalates from polite combat through open combat up to mortal combat, although you or your opponent can disengage at any time.

The key to winning a power struggle is to seem willing to go to any lengths to win and to use a variety of strategies to put your opponent in the submissive position.

Power struggles can end with a clear-cut winner/loser with one person submitting to the other, with a truce—either permanent or temporary—that establishes a peer relationship, or with retreat so you can regroup and fight again.

REBALANCING
THE POWER
IN YOUR LIFE

Power Relationships
and Power Dialects

Now that you're beginning to speak powertalk, you may notice that you're looking at people in a new way. Suddenly, you find you're assessing their powertalk and subtalk. In the process, you'll probably discover there are a lot of subtle variations in the powertalk you hear. These differences are the result of the varying power relationships between people. Powertalkers don't speak to everyone in the same way. Although they never slip into subtalk, they use a more respectful form of powertalk toward those they respect for being on an equal power plane.

Understanding the power relationships you are involved in, and the variations required in your powertalk, can help you become more effective. So let's take a closer look at these relationships, and the brand of powertalk that belongs to each.

There are basically four types of power relationships possible between people, and each one is related to a separate style of powertalk:

Dominance—The mode of speech is powertalk.

Submission—The mode of speech is subtalk.

Codominance—The mode of speech is peertalk positive.

Cosubmission—The mode of speech is peertalk negative.

So far, we have discussed speaking powertalk and avoiding subtalk as means of taking power and gaining the upper hand in relationships. However, this has been an oversimplification that I used to make it easier to teach the basics of powertalk. For the remainder of the book, we are going to learn how to apply powertalk in all the different areas of our lives, and it is important that we do not think of it just as a way of dominating people.

Of course, it is very unpleasant to relate to others submissively. But dominance is a lonely road, and in many situations it is not only isolating but unnecessary, inappropriate, and destructive. Most of the time — with friends, family, lovers, and even colleagues — what we really want is a peer relationship, the kind of respectful equality that comes from a recognition by two people of each other's power.

Unfortunately, we live in a world where personal equality is not always granted automatically. Oftentimes we have to earn it by playing a hard game of powertalk with the other person, showing them that we cannot be dominated. Only after we win their respect will they take us seriously.

This is far from a universal situation. There are many people who are extremely open and civilized, who will extend the hand of equality to you from the first meeting.

It is important to recognize people like this, meet them on their own ground, and speak positive peertalk to them from the start.

Codominance
and Cosubmission

There are two kinds of peer relationships: codominance, and cosubmission.

Codominance is a peer relationship between dominant personalities. It takes place when two people recognize one another as equals in power, eschew the attempt to dominate, and instead decide to socialize, live, or work together cooperatively.

Cosubmission is a peer relationship between submissive personalities. It develops when two or more people who lack power and initiative get together to console one another, complain, and support themselves in self-pity.

You can observe codominant relationships wherever successful people meet as equals. This is not to deny that cosubmissive relationships flourish at the edges of the world of success, while all walks of life have people in them who are successful and powerful, and relate to their peers codominantly.

Co-dominants speak a variation of powertalk called *peertalk positive* with one another. It is a meticulously nonaggressive language. In fact, its primary characteristics are courtesy and deference.

One prototype for peertalk positive is the reception of one head of state or leader of industry by another. The host opens his home, palace, yacht, or whatever to the guest and affords him the utmost in luxury, with the presumption that it is the manner of living to which he is accustomed. The guest accepts graciously, secure that he can reciprocate in kind when his turn comes. In conversation, each vies to be deferential to the other, listening and responding to what he says, and trying to anticipate and meet his needs. This is done without any hint of submission, but with a sense of noblesse oblige.

The other prototype for peertalk positive is that of two companions or equal partners of the same age and sex. Both of these codominants share equally, pay their own way, and take care of their own needs. Neither one offers nor expects any deference, but neither will they tolerate being bossed or dominated in any respect. Their conversation is much less formal and more intimate. There is a more give-and-take exchange, which might include such elements as criticism, unsolicited advice, and teasing. However, there is also a respect for the other person's boundaries and limits.

Both forms of peertalk positive are characterized more by what they exclude, than what they include. First, they exclude all subtalk. Deference, while it exists, is clearly a matter of courtesy, not submissiveness. Second, they exclude the attempt to dominate. While the verbal style is powertalk, it is only used to establish one's own boundaries and prerogatives, not to intrude on those of the other. Third, they exclude direct aggression, which may only be expressed through competition in work, sports and games, and sometimes through humor, but it may never be expressed directly, or allowed to conflict with courtesy. This is even true with codominants who might dislike one another.

Cosubmissives speak in a style called *peertalk negative*.

The prototype for the cosubmissive relationship is two victims who have come together for comfort, washing one another in a bath of rationalization and self-deception. Cosubmissives agree to unconditionally and indiscriminatingly support one another.

In their conversations, cosubmissives complain of the injustices of the world, and the inhumanity of those who mistreat them. They talk about what they will do if pushed far enough. And they fantasize all sorts of improbable solutions: divorces, new jobs, moving to California or New York, which they will resort to in the indeterminate future. They do not take responsibility for their own role in their misfortunes, nor do they look for constructive ways to change their lives, and gain power and respect. In their versions of their lives, they are blameless, unappreciated, misunderstood, and the victims of both other people and circumstances beyond their control.

Instead of helping one another to escape these self-deceptions and to implement real solutions, cosubmissives take turns in supporting each other's fantasies. They speak subtalk to dominant personalities, but they use a very mixed language among themselves. For one thing, they speak a lot of highly aggressive powertalk to imaginary others, with the other person as audience, as they rehash or rehearse what they did or will say to someone who has crossed them.

Typical peertalk negative statements include: "The nerve of him." . . . "I'm going into the office tomorrow and tell her exactly what I think of her." . . . "You shouldn't have to put up with that." . . . "How dare they treat you that way." . . . "I'd like to give him a piece of my mind."

In actuality, peertalk negative reinforces the helplessness of the talkers, fixes the habit of subtalking, and underlines the fact that they think of themselves as followers who are acted upon, rather than leaders who can create change and action by their own power. They may share a depressive, commiserating mood, as they survey a rotten and hopeless situation.

Cosubmissives also speak highly deferential peertalk positive to one another, but they do so erratically. Their purpose in speaking positive peertalk is not to honor the other's power, but rather to build them up, so as to make their approval more significant. Frequently, cosubmissives share a kind of forced hilarity based on finding themselves wonderful, superior, and forgivable in their failings while being hypercritical of those outside their circle.

Cosubmissives place a lot of importance on friendship, loyalty, and human values; they de-emphasize the importance of success, money, and achievement. They use a lot of language from the realms of psychology, ethics and aesthetics.

Cosubmissives make good friends as long as neither tries to change. Since each is involved in the other's passivity and uncritical support, they become a liability if one of their circle tries to change into a more powerful person. If you are a submissive person and a habitual subtalker who decides to become a powertalker, you will have to resign yourself to becoming much less close to your cosubmissive friends. Stop indulging in peertalk negative, and begin replacing your cosubmissive friendships with some more challenging ones.

Rebalancing
the Power in Your Life

The remaining chapters in this book will teach you how to use your new skills at powertalk to rebalance the power in all areas of your life. As you apply them, it is important to keep in mind the four kinds of power relationships we have just discussed. Keep the distinction clear between dominance and codominance. You should usually avoid creating dominant relationships with peers, friends, and lovers, and often with colleagues as well, because the closer the relationship is, the more dominance will erode good feeling and create resentment in its place.

On the other hand, it is usually a mistake to try to have a true peer relationship in situations where one person must dominate the other. Relationships between teachers and students, bosses and subordinates, parents and children are frequently damaged by the well-meant but misguided attempt to establish too much equality.

Powertalk is a tool for establishing the respect necessary to both dominant and codominant relationships. However, if you want to sustain codominant relationships, you must switch from ordinary powertalk to peertalk positive as soon as possible.

Finally, you must be wary of those who extend the hand of friendship, only to use the guise of a peer relationship in order to take advantage of you. Establishing and maintaining really good, equable peer relationships — where neither exploits the other—is a fine art, and one of the most important uses of powertalk.

Arenas of Power

There are three different power arenas in your life:

1. **The personal arena**—friendships, love relationships, children, and relatives. There's a considerable amount of powertalk and subtalk in this area of life, which may be making your relationships less satisfying than they can be.

2. **The outside world**—officials, professionals, bureaucrats, clerks, even waiters. Some of these people may elicit automatic subtalk from you and then needlessly frustrate and complicate your life.

3. **The business world**—employers, coworkers, subordinates, clients and customers, and suppliers. Inadequate powertalk may give you trouble in selling, maintaining authority, and getting work done. Powertalk problems not only interfere with your ability

to function on the job, but may have serious long-
term effects, such as slowing or even stopping your
advancement and earning potential.

In each of these arenas, your powertalk must be slightly
different. For example, because of your intimate knowledge in your personal relationships, you have enormous
capacity to cause hurt during a powertalk encounter. By
misusing these potent weapons, you would defeat your
very objective of realigning the relationship.

In contrast, your main concern with bureaucrats is to
get what you want. You'll never see these people again,
which probably won't matter to you anyway. Yet you
have no knowledge of these people to use in powertalk
encounters and all power struggles will undoubtedly take
place on your opponents' territory under their terms.
Clearly, the situation is so different that powertalk must
change as well.

In each area, the amount of power you hold may also be
different, dictating a special strategy. For instance, you
may hold considerable power at work that you can use to
back up your powertalk. As a result, you primarily use
straight powertalk; when you make threats, everyone
knows without saying that you have the authority to back
them. However, on the home front, your father remains in
stern, tight control of his extended family, insisting that
all of his children gather at his home regularly and live in
accordance with his fairly comprehensive dictates. His
control is such that he can threaten anyone who mis-
behaves with exclusion from the entire family unit—and
since this is the core of your personal life as a child, you're
not willing to risk expulsion. In this situation, your power
base is limited. Powertalk game plans are virtually a
necessity, and your strategies must be very carefully plot-
ted.

The following chapters focus on different tasks and

problems selected from a variety of power arenas. They will give you specific guidance, but even more, they will provide examples in how to think through powertalk problems, and find appropriate solutions to them. By studying them, you will make it much easier to solve your own powertalk problems.

Finding
Your Power Vacuums

As I pointed out in the beginning, some of us are basically powertalkers, and some are basically subtalkers; however, within this there is a lot of variation. All our personalities are comprised of a number of roles, and we use separate roles in different situations and relationships. In some of our roles, we might be highly dominant and use a lot of powertalk; in others, the opposite is true.

When you took the PQ test in Chapter 2, you answered the questions in a general way, and they gave you a general sense of your powertalk quotient. Now I am going to suggest that you retake this test—not once but several times. You can take it for each role that you customarily play in your life: spouse, parent, employee, team member, patient, and so on. Whenever you take it for a particular role, answer the questions regarding how you specifically act in that role. You will probably find this easier than taking the test the first time, when you had to balance your behavior in a number of roles to come up with a general answer.

Just what will you get out of this? Each time you take it for a different role, you will get a reading on just how dominant or submissive you are. If you take it for all the major roles in your life, and compare the scores, you will get a profile of your entire life. Areas of low scores will point out where you are habitually submissive, and where you have to apply powertalk to change your relationships.

On the other hand, areas of very high scoring may indicate problems as well. Subtalkers, as well as powertalkers, often overcompensate for their pervasive submissiveness and become domineering in situations where they feel relatively strong (for example, with children or subordinates). If you find areas where your PQ is very high, examine them carefully, and make sure they are not areas where you are unwittingly becoming a bully.

Expect Resistance When You Try to Change Existing Relationships

Most people don't like it when a comfortable, established relationship changes in any way. This is particularly true when the established relationship gives the other person most or all of the power. In a few cases, a direct discussion using straight powertalk will be sufficient. But all too often, you're going to meet with resistance, sometimes extremely strong resistance. A single encounter will frequently be insufficient. It's important to stay focused on why you want the relationship changed and stick with your efforts. In between power struggle episodes, there may be quiet periods when you and your opponent function normally. Don't slip back into subtalk! Once you demand a new power relationship, you must sustain your strive to peertalk/powertalk mix at all times, even when you're not actively struggling for power. This will have a cumulative impact on your opponent, eventually forcing him or her to see you in a different, more powerful way. If you slip into subtalk, your opponent will rightly conclude that you're not really determined to change the relationship, and not powerful enough to force him or her to treat you differently.

Summary

There are four types of power relationships between people . . . dominance, submission, codominance, and cosubmission.

When you are dominant you speak powertalk.

When you are submissive you speak subtalk.

When you are codominant you speak peertalk positive.

When you are cosubmissive you speak peertalk negative.

Codominance and cosubmission are both peer relationships.

Codominance is a peer relationship between two people who are habitually dominant, but have decided to share power instead of contesting it.

Cosubmission is a relationship between two people who are habitually submissive, and reinforce one another's submissiveness. It is an undesirable relationship.

You will have to understand all of these relationships and how they are used to really rebalance the power in your life.

For instance you should avoid creating dominant relationships with friends and lovers.

On the other hand it is usually a bad idea to try for a codominant relationship where the situation dictates a dominant relationship, such as between teacher and student, or employer and employee.

Deciding on the appropriate relationship and establishing it is one of powertalk's finer arts.

POWERTALK
AND THE OUTSIDE
WORLD
10

Almost every day, people you hardly know and may never see again create delays, unnecessary work, problems, and frustration by powertalking to you. Wouldn't it be nice to get fast attention from waiters and government clerks, avoid traffic tickets, deal with doctors and lawyers on a more equal footing? You can—with powertalk!

The reason you're usually submissive to these people is because you perceive an assymetrical relationship. You recognize that they have a power center based upon their professional qualifications or institutional alliances. You forget that you also possess a power base—you are either a purchaser of their services, which means you can take your money elsewhere, or you're a taxpayer and therefore indirectly the one who pays the salaries of the very people who are powertalking to you. Even when you recognize this, you hesitate to use powertalk because you fear these people have the ability to make trouble for you. But that's a subtalker's attitude and it gets the kind of results you'd expect—dominance, indifference, and a disregard of your needs and feelings. Powertalk, adapted to the situation of course, is the only way to achieve what you want.

How to Get Respect from the Wise Professionals

Doctors, dentists, and lawyers are almost universally powertalkers who totally dominate their patients and clients. Doctors use the classic technique of addressing you by your first name while you respectfully say, "Yes, Dr. Smith."

Doctors and dentists assume they know best about your physical well-being. They may even assume they know best about your psychological state and presume to offer additional advice about matters entirely out of their expertise. In particular, they usually assume you have little ability to make medical or health judgments—you can tell them how you feel but your interpretations may be ignored. Any knowledge you may have about treatments, diagnoses, the dangers of X-rays, nutrition, or other matters might even be dismissed out of hand. To preserve your ignorance, they may tell you very little, complicated with jargon (so you feel ignorant). They are often unresponsive to questions, and frequently seem to feel threatened by any attempt on your part to control your own treatment.

How does it work? A friend of mine with severe high-blood pressure complained regularly to her doctor that the medication was making her sleep too much, feel fuzzy-headed and no longer alert or sharp, and generally giving her a drugged sensation. She repeatedly asked that the doctor try reducing the dosage of the pills that were causing it (she was taking three different drugs). Each time, the doctor patted her on the shoulder and murmured that she had to accept these minor discomforts for the sake of her health, at the same time implying that her complaints might be imaginary.

Finally, my friend developed a fever, a symptom the doctor couldn't ignore and he took her off that medication completely. Her other problems disappeared within forty-eight hours and her blood pressure remained under control! She's still bitterly angry at having endured a year of feeling constantly sick for no reason.

Use powertalk to establish an open relationship with your doctor. Find out what's going on by continuing to ask questions. When the doctor tries to give you jargon, ask for a translation. If the doctor indicates you've taken up too much time, cross your legs, sit back, and ask some more questions. Force him or her to give you complete information, to explain why something is being "recommended," (you retain the final decision). Get complete information on side effects and drawbacks. Make it quite clear that you're ready to do research to check on the information and that for anything serious, you'll get another opinion.

If your doctor calls you by your first name, do the same to him or her. If your doctor takes endless phone calls in the middle of examining you, start getting dressed, pick up your file, and start reading it or make a few calls of your own, moving into his private office to do so if he's using the phone in the examining room. Another strategy might be to have your office or a friend posing as your office call you half a dozen times while you're at the doctor's, and keep him waiting while you apparently deal with crises too critical to wait. End your conversations with important statements, for example: "That's going to have to wait until I get back there. I'll be back in . . . (to the doctor) how long would you say this is going to take?"

If your doctor is famous for putting you into examining rooms, making you get undressed, and then leaving you alone for what seems like hours, refuse to go. Tell the nurse to let you know when the doctor's really ready for you, or start marching up and down the hall in the little examining gown, peeking into other rooms and yelling, "Hey, Doc, where are you?" as if playing hide and seek.

If your doctor keeps you waiting for hours, make an issue of the fact that you don't want to wait when you make the appointment. Call before you leave for the appointment to see if he or she is running on schedule. When you arrive, announce that you must leave in forty-five minutes — exactly. Every five minutes of waiting time, tell the receptionist or nurse the exact time that you have to leave.

All these devices are designed not just to get action but to show the doctor that you are as important as he or she is and your time is as valuable. Because of the authoritative position of medical people you've got to make the point in a strong way, so don't hesitate to use a little "unmitigated gall!"

While talking with your physician or dentist, avoid overly deferential language as well. Treat him or her as an equal, ask questions about personal matters, or give advice (for example, "Ever been to Palm Springs, Bob? I just got back and what a place! You've got to go there. Listen, tell you what, when you go, let me know and I'll set it up so you can play tennis at the Whatsis Club").

Hospitals

Hospitals combine the worst of the bureaucracy with the worst of the medical profession. They can reduce you to a powerless infant before you've gotten settled in your bed. Ironically, although the entire hospital operation is geared to transforming you into a bed number, hospital nurses and medical professionals will tell you that the best way to get good care in a hospital is to actively participate in your treatment. Almost every patient can tell tales of errors, and nurses who become patients question every medication before taking it, demand specific treatments, and even refuse some. So even if you feel like a submissive child during your hospital stay, it's in your own best interests to keep on powertalking!

Hospital staffs are not only experts in treating you like a baby, but they're overworked, which means the squeaky wheel gets the most attention. Gentle powertalk is usually ineffective. You need to use strong, demanding, intimidating powertalk.

- Insist on knowing the cost of things. One woman was unable to get her doctor to discuss a problem she had with her hospitalization. The doctor finally tried to put her down by saying, "How much is your life worth?" She answered, "About $55, if I can't get coverage. Shall I cancel the operation or can we deal with this matter now?" He dealt with it.

- Demand to know precisely what's happening. A friend of mine had a diagnostic test which resulted in agonizing spasms for days afterwards, but no one told her the spasms were a side effect. Instead, they gave her drugs when the pain became unbearable and pushed aside any questions about what was causing it. Finally, she informed the nurse that she insisted on knowing what was happening. The nurse said her doctor was away for the weekend, so she called his answering service and told them to tell the doctor that if he didn't get in touch with her within a half hour she was walking out of the hospital. Five minutes later, the nurse hurried into her room to tell her the doctor was on the phone to the nurse's station and would be calling her momentarily.

- Insist on complete information. When the doctor visits, ask questions. Demand that he draw a diagram of the surgery, ask about the side effects, alternatives, and recuperative treatments. Sign nothing without asking about everything you don't understand. Position yourself as a participant in the treatment and use the threat of complete refusal if you do not get the consideration you require.

● Refuse to be ignored or mistreated. If aides start talking as if they were alone in the room, tell them to leave, and if they don't, create a scene. If you don't get attention, go to higher-ups, and make scenes. (In the middle of the night, one patient who couldn't get a nurse called the switchboard and demanded the home number of the hospital administrator. She didn't get the number but she did get the nurse.)

● Don't permit yourself to be treated like a kid at a boarding school. Many hospital rules are established to make things easy for the staff. Question them; if there isn't a good reason, ignore them. Sleep when you feel the need. Open your window or change the temperature setting in your room. Get dressed when you want. Have friends bring your meals in from other sources. (I know one patient who even got the nurses to heat up her private stock of food on their personal hotplate.) Force the staff to treat you as a person.

Lawyers

Lawyers also act superior but in a different way. They feel quite sure they're more intelligent and better educated than you. They assume that since they represent you in an area where you're incompetent, they're entitled to make all decisions—and to advise you on other matters as well.

Lawyers may try to make you paranoid, to give you the feeling that everyone but them is out to get you. They also may attempt to instill greediness in you. They rob you of your power by refusing to let you talk directly to any of the other parties, and by taking definitive actions when you're not even around.

Retain your power by making it quite clear at the out-set that you are buying your lawyer's services, and that you're in charge. Refuse to go "on the clock" (paying by the hour) and negotiate a definite fee for the job. Insist on a review of all expenses that will be charged in addition to the fee, explain *your* conditions for the relationship, i.e., Phone calls must be returned promptly. You expect regular reports covering all details. You will not accept any decisions made without your prior approval or in your absence. Don't let your attorney resort to jargon to prevent your involvement. Demand full information and explanations right down the line.

Dealing with the Pompous Powerless _____

Clerks, waiters, sales people, and lower-level bureaucrats are essentially powerless people very near the bottom of their power structures. Often they dislike their jobs as well. So they put a little "fun" into their jobs, and create a feeling of power by powertalking you, the person who needs their attention, and making things difficult for you. Those who work for powerful institutions play the Lord's servant game. Waiters and sales people play snob, suggesting that they're doing you a favor by serving you. The usual feeling is that if you're nice to these people, they'll recognize you're one of the few nice ones and cooperate with you. Actually, having successfully intimidated you, they will be more contemptuous.

Act As if You're Used to Having Servants ___

The best approach to service people and clerks is to treat them like your servants—not bullying or crude (this reveals your fear and lack of assurance) but with calm, courtesy, and the assumption that your slightest wish will be met.

If this doesn't work, here are a few suggestions:

The Department of Motor Vehicles and Other Government Agencies

If the line is long, make yours a special case that requires you go to the supervisor, then powertalk the supervisor into handling your entire procedure for you (the way a bank manager handles deposits for a new account). Clerks follow very rigid rules so it's not too difficult to raise a question or phrase your problem in a way that requires contact with the supervisor. You don't really care how flimsy it is anyway since you only want an excuse to approach the supervisor and sit down. Once seated, you can shift into your tight time constraints, the influential people you know, and the other reasons why the supervisor should expedite handling your problem.

If you've waited on line only to be turned down because of a minor rule, don't take no for an answer. Relax and rest against the counter as if you've got all day. Say, "You don't understand," and repeat your demands. If the clerk still refuses, say, "Perhaps I haven't explained myself clearly" and repeat your demands again. Keep on doing so —very courteously—until the clerk gives in. If the clerk starts to get angry instead, say, "I just can't accept that. How do we get this through?" Then try to negotiate your demands. If that's not possible, ask for the supervisor.

The Internal Revenue Service

One tax consultant suggests that if you're in a position where an audit is likely, prepare for it by making a few errors on your returns that would give you credits. If the first thing the IRS auditor finds merits a refund to you, chances are likely that he or she will quickly conclude the audit.

If you're called before you can prepare this advance strategy, you've got several other options. One highly successful woman goes to audits with shopping bags filled with miscellaneous jumbles of receipts and records, then starts spreading everything over the auditor's desk, muttering, "Oh, yes, I can document that; just wait a second." If the auditor tries to switch to something else (as a way of stopping the clutter and managing time), she refuses, saying, "No, no, I've got it; let me just go through this bag now." Visualizing an audit that could take months and net close to nothing, the auditor quickly gives up.

This sort of approach can even be improved upon if you act slightly hysterical and obsessed with the most minute details. Another option is to outplay the auditor at his or her own game while acting like the most buttoned-down IRS auditor. To do this, act very legalistic, speak with great precision, have every proof fully organized (preferably in excessively neat records with small notes to yourself on every receipt), know every law, and force the auditor to listen to detailed explanations for every point.

You can even use negative powertalk and enter the auditor's office in tears, shaking with anxiety. Before the auditor has said a thing, ask if they have a ten-year plan for paying off penalties. Your excessive fear will make you look honest and your question about time payments signals that collecting anything out of you is going to be rather difficult.

Generally, if you have a weak case, play a role that shows you as being honest, broke, incompetent at figures, and totally disorganized. If you have a strong case, bring numerous records and offer lengthy explanations for the most minute items.

Waiters

Act as if you're used to the best in service and treat the staff in restaurants as if you had a full staff at home. Never indicate you're worried about money. (If you sit down only to find the prices are too steep, comment, "For the type of menu offered, I think it's overpriced.")

If the restaurant is very snobbish, play the wine and gourmet game harder than the staff does, but be sure they don't discover your guise. Ask questions they don't know, or ask questions that indicate discrimination. For instance, "Are the *tournedos* made with onions or shallots?" . . . "Does the chef make the pasta here?" . . . "Do you get your truffles direct from France?" . . . "Is the fish made with fresh or dried tarragon? I hate the taste of dried tarragon."

When you don't get service, speak loudly and threaten to make a real scene. A complaint will get faster attention than a request for service. A loud statement, such as, "Waiter, I think this salad dressing is rancid" will bring everyone running! At the same time, don't make absurd demands—they only make you look silly and uneducated. Acting as if you expect gourmet service at MacDonald's is not powertalk but merely ignorant. Play the game on whatever level is consonant with your surroundings. A power person should be at ease in all situations.

Store Clerks

Store clerks are very much like waiters. Play the game harder than they do. If they're total snobs, outsnob them by treating them like your servants. If you can't get their attention, use a loud demanding voice and create a problem. For instance, "Miss, is this a real Givenchy? It looks fake."

In grocery stores, voice your complaint loud enough to be heard by the manager, and accompany it with a threat. For example, "Obviously, customers interfere with your work; I'll take my business somewhere else."

General rules for clerks: Never go in person if you can telephone (you usually get more attention from a higher-level employee). Use celebrity influence. Clerks are almost always impressed by celebrities. If you can refer to any that you know, you'll attach yourself to a VIP level immediately.

Sometimes acting as if you're a secretary or assistant to someone powerful can get more assistance—it puts you more or less on the clerk's level and allows you to invoke the authority of your boss, to refuse to take no for an answer ("I'm so afraid of what he'll do if I tell him that").

Powertalk and the Power of the Law _____

Never try tough powertalk on a cop!

The best strategy when stopped for a traffic violation or some other minor infraction is to approach the police officer as a middle-class citizen (a taxpayer and not a member of the criminal classes) who is courteous but not obsequious or submissive. Don't make the problem into a personal issue or try to use hostility. The police have an almost automatic response to hostility that requires them to react with great power.

Since the police are accustomed to a barrage of excuses, a different response that creates a mutual acknowledgment that the two of you are human beings can sometimes result in a lighter penalty. "You got me," said one powertalker ruefully. "Bad car!" said another, hitting the dashbord. "Why do you always go so fast!" "I knew I was pushing my luck when I finished that great mystery yesterday instead of getting the car inspected," said a third. In all instances, the officer responded with a chuckle and a warning.

_____Summary_____

The world is full of situations where other people try to establish inappropriate dominance over you. Your task is to combat this. In order to do this you must establish your power base, and compel them to recognize and respect it.

When physicians, dentists, and hospital personnel try to powertalk you, force them to answer all your questions, reply in kind to being addressed by your first name, let them know you are important, and use tactics to make it difficult for them to keep you waiting for an inordinate length of time, or otherwise take advantage of you.

With attorneys, set the ground rules and negotiate all fees in advance.

Don't let clerks, waiters, and sales people give you the snob treatment. If they try, treat them with the perfect courtesy with which the upper classes have always treated servants.

When dealing with the IRS, either overwhelm them with over-documentation and precision or with the sheer chaos of your record keeping.

Never try to powertalk cops. Talk to them with respect, but in a dignified way. Humor sometimes helps.

POWERTALK
BETWEEN FAMILY,
FRIENDS, AND LOVERS

▌▐

Changing the power balance with people who are emotionally important to you requires a certain amount of delicacy and special care. It is highly unlikely that you want to be a heavy-handed dictator in intimate relationships. And you certainly don't want to jeopardize the future of your relationships by overwhelming people.

At the same time, people in personal relationships are often rigidly entrenched in their respective roles and take the current power balance for granted. Any effort to change things is likely to be met with fierce resistance. The power struggle will probably be a campaign. And because of your intimate relationship with people, you'll have to be especially alert to renewals of the power struggle at unexpected times . . . and the damage you can do to your power struggle by slipping into subtalk at any time.

General Rules for Powertalking People You Care About

There are several basics that apply to power changes with anyone in the personal area of your life:

1. *Choose topics of conversation for your powertalk struggles with great care.* Some subjects can be destructive to the entire relationship. Because of your knowledge of the other person, you can inflict devastating damage and force him or her into fighting to the bitter end, ripping your relationship to shreds in the process. The more personal and intimate the topic, the more dangerous it is as a powertalk battle. Innocuous issues are generally safer. In other words, the president's economic policy may well be a better subject for a power struggle with your spouse than your sexual practices.

   People are most defensive about personal issues that define them as individuals. Avoid engaging in a power struggle that revolves around the following topics:

   - individual sexual practices and desires

   - personal cleanliness and/or grooming

   - values, ethics, and morality

   - talents and skills in critical areas of a person's life (a mother's talent as a mother, for instance)

   - personal habits, particularly those revealed to very few people

2. *Be as specific as possible about what is wrong.* Often you will be tempted to be general about an issue in order to avoid head-on collisions, but this is almost always a mistake. Being vague and general is a bad

strategy for trying to accomplish changes in a relationship. Generalities lead to misunderstandings. If you make vague statements, the other person is likely to assume that you are talking about different things.

When people are criticized in nonspecific ways, they invariably fill in the blanks with things they are sensitive about. Then they become defensive, overreact, and either withdraw or take the offensive. All of these responses tend to turn discussions into arguments.

The problem becomes even worse when you carry on a general discussion, at the end of which everyone agrees in a general way to try harder, and do things differently. At first you feel better, but since you were never really talking about the same things in the first place, no real change has occurred. Sooner or later the person starts powertalking you in a way you thought he or she agreed to give up. In addition to your usual displeasure you feel angry that the agreement has been betrayed. Then you are likely to attack them. This starts up a battle that soon makes it impossible to return to the subject and renegotiate it calmly.

The world is littered with marriages that have failed because people didn't know how to negotiate instead of fight. They became erroneously convinced that their spouses were unwilling to change and grant them more equality.

3. *Point out things when they are happening.* Do this as calmly and nonaccusingly as possible; if the time is inopportune, wait until it is right to talk about it.

4. *Try open, straight discussion, before you resort to strategies.* While this might not always be successful, it is the safest and most respectful approach, and should always be tried first. For example: "You

know, darling, I really am happy to share the driving on these long trips, but I don't like it when you constantly back-seat drive, telling me how fast to go, and pointing out signs and lights. If you want me to drive, I insist you let me do it my way. Why don't you just close your eyes and take a rest? Everything will be fine."

5. *Never tell an intimate what they should do.* This sets you up as a moral authority. If the other person has any backbone at all, it will invariably put their back up and elicit retorts such as, "Nobody tells me what to do." . . . "Who are you to give orders?"

6. *Give people room to be generous and come to you.* Never push your argument and your authority so far that the other person feels they are giving in, and losing both ground and face. Let them feel good about coming around instead, and then thank them for being so fair and open-minded. However, don't expect them to come around until you let them know they really have no choice. People may act nobly, but they usually don't give up ground unless they see it is inevitable.

7. *Avoid anger, ultimatums, and harsh criticism.* Try appealing to their better side with pleasantness, reason, and sometimes, humor.

8. *Expect a certain amount of unpleasant resistance whenever you try to change a power relationship.* People will counter in all sorts of ways: nastiness, sarcasm, criticism, threats of withdrawal and abandonment, accounts of all they have done for you, and so on. Of course, it is unfair and insufferable, and the only self-respecting response is to put an end to it the moment they get started. However, if you respond that way, you will lose far more relationships than you change.

Keep in mind that you are asking them to give up some power to you, and that even though it is fair, they still will experience it as a setback and a loss. You will be far more successful if you can absorb and neutralize some flak, particularly at the beginning, and keep coming back to your point in a nice way.

Of course, there is a limit, and it varies depending on how important the relationship is to you. You will have to decide each case individually. Don't go overboard with your newfound power, and alienate a lot of people you will wish you had back.

9. *Stick to your guns.* People are not going to give up accustomed power quickly or easily. Keep to your demands for more equality over a long period of time. What's more, you are going to have to do it consistently, because any hesitation will be perceived as indecision, and will lead them to resist harder. The longer you must keep at it, the more important it is to do it in a nice manner. If not, things will eventually deteriorate.

Power with Your Friends

Who does favors for whom? Who waits and who is always late for meetings? Who decides where you'll go, what you'll do, when you'll do it? Who listens to whose problems? Who runs errands, lends things, gives more expensive gifts? If there's a marked split in any of these situations, you and your friend have a power imbalance. And friendship can be richer, more satisfying, and more enjoyable between equals.

Exactly how you go about changing the power balance depends upon the kind of power relationship you have now. Friendship comes in many different varieties, as evidenced in the following descriptions.

Building an Equal Relationship with a Powerful Friend

Even though your friend has a great deal more real power than you, you'd like to stop dancing at attendance, and establish more equality between yourselves. To do this, you have to convince your friend that you now hold enough power to merit upgrading the power balance. Since people tend to stop looking at subtle changes after they get to know each other, you need to force your friend to look at you again in a new light. Here's how:

- Identify your power bases and start talking confidently about them whenever you're with your friend. Don't hesitate to switch the conversation back to your power bases repeatedly. You've got to push hard to make your friend recognize that you now claim power.

  One woman I know had an older friend all through high school and college, and the relationship evolved around the older one giving the younger one advice. As the younger friend advanced in her career, the role of taking advice began to rankle, and she wanted a completely equal relationship. However, her friend couldn't seem to make the adjustment. Finally, she hit on a scheme and invited her friend and her fiancé to accompany her to a gala dinner that her company was sponsoring, saying nothing more than she had gotten a couple of extra tickets and it was bound to be great fun. When she was introduced as the keynote speaker, she just smiled as if it was nothing out of the ordinary. When she returned to the table, their relationship had changed.

- Offer expertise and counsel to your friend, based upon your power base(s). For instance, suppose you've done a great deal of traveling in your life even though you're a legal secretary with a relatively low income, small home, and few other claims to status. Your friend is a leader in her field, earns an enormous amount of money, and has two homes. You've always been the submissive admirer in the relationship. *Use* your travel expertise—tell your friend where to go on vacation, provide the names of little-known sights and entertainments, offer the addresses of friends in these faraway places. Focus the conversation on unusual anecdotes of your trips.

- Stop acting like a subordinate. Don't be grateful for the things power people do for subordinates. Reciprocate favors.

- Introduce your friend to *your* subordinates and admirers.

Your friend has a vested interest in not perceiving your growth, so you must use strong, clear signals and forceful powertalk to put on pressure.

Stop Talking Peertalk Negative _____

If you and your friend have been weakening one another by offering the support of peertalk negative, you can't just switch over to peertalk positive. Your friend is a habitual subtalker; just because you can now speak powertalk, it doesn't mean your friend can do so. In fact, your friend may feel your sudden lack of sympathy for the lot of the powerless is a betrayal and abandonment.

A friendship based upon peertalk negative requires radical readjustment. You may not be able to turn this friend into a peer; establishing a dominant/subordinate relationship may be your only option, if you wish to preserve any part of the friendship.

One thing is clear: You must change this relationship around because it's weakening and destructive to you, and will damage any efforts to speak powertalk in other parts of your life. You cannot share powerlessness with a friend and still feel like a person of power. At best, you can take the role of the strong listener and advisor. Precisely what kind of relationship you can establish depends to a great extent on the other person. Perhaps your friend is ready to be gradually helped to a position of greater power—in which case, you take the role of mentor and share this book. Or maybe your friend simply won't get out of the subtalking rut, forcing you to take a very dominant position. Whatever is necessary—STOP TALKING PEERTALK NEGATIVE!

Stop a Power Fight, and Establish a Positive Peer Relationship

Sometimes power struggles go on for years, with periodic truces and occasional sharp battles but never a final, complete resolution. This sort of relationship isn't a good foundation for trusting, caring, or the other benefits of friendship. Maybe it's time to stop playing power games and discuss the power relationship with straight powertalk. To stop a fight that's been going on for a very long time, it's absolutely vital that you, first of all, acknowledge that you're both worthy adversaries who fight well. Second, stop trying to dominate (that means *you stop*, right now). Third, stick to very open, honest discussion.

Select a time when your friend is most open to a frank talk, when you're certain to have ample opportunity to fully discuss your difficulty without interruption. Stick to straight powertalk (or better, straight peertalk) and bring any of your friend's effort to switch to a power game out in the open. Once you achieve an acknowledgment of the problem and your friend agrees that you should be peers, continue the discussion until you have clearly outlined the way your relationship will be conducted.

Powertalk and Love

Powertalk often undergoes major transformations in love relationships, but it still exists, even in the beautiful blossoming of romance. In fact, powertalk changes in each of the four basic stages of a love relationship:

1. Meeting a Potential Lover_____

During the meeting phase of a relationship, the person who does the pursuing has less power than the pursued one. Thus, a pursuer who is very casual and cool—almost uncaring—is playing a powertalk game, trying to retain the power edge. Alternatively, the pursuer may try to move the relationship along very quickly to a point where he or she can regain the dominant role. (Ironically, in terms of real power, the pursuer has the edge since he or she can stop pursuing at any time, but this portion of the meeting phase doesn't last long. The moment the pursuer shows that winning the affections and attentions of the pursued one is important, he or she becomes the less powerful one in the relationship.)

One major change in powertalk is that "dirty talk" is often used as a part of testing the readiness of the other person for a physical advance. Dirty jokes, innuendoes, double meanings, and other verbal parries are initiated by one party; if the other person laughs or responds favorably, he or she signals interest and availability. This can turn into a combination power game/courtship ritual when a powertalker responds to the dirty talk, then turns around and acts incensed at the physical advances that follow. A skilled powertalker who is more interested in controling another person than really getting involved in a deep relationship may tease like this repeatedly, gaining the upper hand by creating confusion until the other person decides to wait until the powertalker clearly tells him or her what to do.

In today's society, some meetings are focused on very

short-term sexual encounters without a real love affair. At best, these encounters involve abrupt, blunt peertalk in which each party tells the other what is wanted from the relationship. Frequently, one person is powertalked into bed by the other. At these times, the powertalker employs the tactics of coercion, persuasion, initiating action, and even intimidation—using a power role instead of his or her own full personality. Sex, in these cases, is a kind of ultimate dominance/submission gesture.

2. Courtship Is an Effort to Obtain Mutual Commitment

During the courtship stage of a love relationship, the pursuer tries to obtain an emotional commitment and involvement from the pursued one. The pursued one, on the other hand, seeks to maintain the upper hand by withholding involvement as long as possible—unless a positive peertalk relationship exists.

In bygone eras, the power relationships in courtship were very clear—and just about the only time women held the position of power. Women dominated by refusing a physical relationship until they obtained a full commitment of marriage from the men. Unfortunately, once the women gave in and went to bed with the men, the men took over complete dominance.

Although sexual intimacy is no longer the pivotal element of courtship, a power struggle still takes place most of the time. These days, the key issue is emotional commitment to one another and to the relationship. The pursuer (who may be either sex) is the first to reveal a deep emotional feeling.

Power struggles between lovers in the courtship stage are very similar to power struggles in any other area of life. Ideally, both parties are honest about their feelings and express a kind of peertalk where they accept one another as equals. Often, however, there is a true battle for dominance:

- Since the pursuer has revealed the depth of his or her feeling and thus become the weaker of the two, he or she may withdraw immediately after the revelation by failing to call, breaking a date, standing up a date, taking someone else out and/or behaving very cooly. The purpose is to make the pursued one uncertain about the accuracy of the revelation and perhaps force him or her to declare mutual feelings of love.

- When the pursued one senses the pursuer's interest is flagging, he or she may give in just a little in order to raise hopes (for instance, by saying, "I'm really starting to care about you").

- Lovers may use powertalk game plans and strategies to gain ascendency. Clear powertalk plays include comments like, "I love the way you get so involved in your little hobbies." (This diminishes the fact that you're the national chairperson of a major charity; he or she is trying to force you to sacrifice your interests for his or hers.) Far too often, the goal of powertalking a lover is to win his or her complete commitment, requiring that the subordinate lover give up anything else he or she cares about, and adopt the other's friends, interests, and concerns. This is usually a complete mockery of the respect and continual refreshment that's vital to any close relationship.

- Lovers may also reveal a desire to be submissive by speaking subtalk in a love relationship. For instance, "Honey, do you love me as much as I love you?" . . . "What do you think I should wear tonight, dear?" . . . "I'm happy being with you wherever we go." . . . "Whatever you want to do is fine with me." This kind of lovetalk invites establishment of an excessively dominant/subordinate relationship, and doesn't portend a happy future. Sometimes women in particular believe that using this language will "build up" their men and help them become more powerful in all aspects of their lives. Actually, it doesn't.

3. Mutual Caring Is Ideally a Peertalk Positive Relationship

When the courted one finally expresses true commitment and feeling, love moves into a new phase. During the early stages, both lovers may use an ornate form of peertalk in which each bends over backwards to display deference, concern, and caring for the other person. Accidental interruptions are followed by effusive apologies, as are any of the other powertalk plays for conversational control. Each lover may try to defer to the other. For example:

> **LOVER 1:** *Whatever you want to do tonight is fine.*
> **LOVER 2:** *No, no, it doesn't matter to me; what do you want?*
> **LOVER 1:** *Honestly, I really want to do what you want.*
> **LOVER 2:** *Well, you did say you wanted to see this movie.*
> **LOVER 1:** *Oh, but you were really interested in the hockey game, weren't you?*
> **LOVER 2:** *Hockey isn't that important to me.*

This is a healthy phase as long as it moves into a more relaxed form of positive peertalk and not a power struggle. The primary goals at this stage of a relationship, to communicate affection, caring, concern, and mutual respect, are demonstrated by this elaborate peertalk.

Generally, this language is accompanied by action—a constructive concern for the other person, establishment of a role in the other person's life, providing feedback, reinforcement, assistance. As time goes on and the peer-talk becomes more natural, the action part of the relationship becomes stronger and more constant. But despite the magical qualities of mutual caring, this stage can still be a power struggle if one or more of the parties are very dominant powertalkers. When one person seeks to make his or her concerns the most important, establish him- or herself as the one who gives advice, initiates action and/or sets the opinions and attitudes for the couple, there's a power struggle. And even though emotions are intense and warm, the other person must resist such efforts and avoid slipping into subtalk if the relationship is to have a future on an equal footing.

4. Established Relationships Should Include Definition of Each Person's Rights _____

The final stage of a love relationship is a long-term commitment (living together or marriage). If the relationship is to be a harmonious peer union, it's important to clearly establish the parameters of personal responsibility (how much freedom each has to come and go, socialize, when and what you eat, retention of friends) and the contractual limitation areas of the relationship (sexual and romantic fidelity, how you'll be available to one another and when). Unless these matters are discussed openly and honestly, they remain possible arenas for future power struggles.

Powertalk and Marriage

It's often difficult to look at a couple and determine who is dominant and who is submissive, although it's usually pretty clear when the couple has a true peer relationship (the mutual courtesy, concern, respect, and sharing are quite obvious). It's even possible to be in a marriage and not be certain how much power you have. (That's why the PQ test in Chapter 2 is so important. It will tell you concretely whether you're the powertalker or the subtalker in a relationship.)

A peer relationship in marriage is based on the existence of separate responsibilities or power centers within the relationship. Within the power center, the individual is free to make unilateral decisions on how to carry out his or her responsibilities. For instance, within reason, the one responsible for maintaining the home should be free to determine how and when to clean and which products to use. In addition, that person should have the right to establish rules about tidiness. (By the way, one of the problems with sharing housekeeping responsibilities is that often the wife who insists on the sharing tries to retain power by telling the husband how and when to clean. If the responsibility is shared, each person should have the right to make decisions independently.)

In areas where both spouses must share the work, considerable attention has to be given to reciprocity, and some degree of agreement on how matters are to be decided should be made in advance. In the personal or intimate sphere of marriage, decisions about lovemaking, play, and personal services should be reciprocated and never coercive. Central areas like where you live, religious practice, and deploying the family finances should be negotiated with consideration for all parties concerned.

Changing an Existing Power Balance _____

Suppose you're already in a marriage in which your spouse has the lion's share of power. Your goal is to change the balance, ideally to a peer relationship. As with friends, the first step should be an attempt to have a straight powertalk/peertalk—a reasonable discussion about the relationship and the power imbalance.

If this doesn't work, the problem is often that your spouse

is so used to viewing you as a weaker person that he or she is not seeing you clearly. What's needed is a campaign that will make your spouse take a new look and see the changes in you. Start by ceasing to speak subtalk (not even as a strategy) and refusing to ask for your spouse's approval or authorization of your opinions and ideas. This can be a calm assertion without argument. (These slight changes will at the very least make your spouse feel you've somehow become a stronger person.)

Next, solidify your power centers within the relationship. No matter how domineering your spouse is, there are areas within your relationship for which you're responsible. Assume that responsibility and resist your spouse's efforts to make decisions that affect them. Again, don't incite argument—calmly use straight peertalk, saying, for instance, "You don't have to worry about that; it's my responsibility."

At this stage, your spouse should be changing his or her view of you rather extensively. So try once again to have a straight peertalk discussion. If your spouse agrees, be sure to fully discuss all areas of your relationship, emphasizing the need for mutual consideration, reciprocity, and negotiation. It might be helpful to write down your agreements to forestall future power struggles and disagreements.

If your spouse again refuses to talk to you about this, or tries to turn the discussion into a power struggle, it's time to enter into the struggle as another powertalker. As with any power struggle between loved ones, certain topics should be avoided or touched upon only with great care. Some powertalk strategies work well between spouses, while others court disaster. A good topic for a power battle is the laws you're entitled to set down because of your responsibilities within the relationship.

One of the most dangerous and destructive issues is to try to dominate the marriage by claiming an outside authority. This rather desperate ploy is frequently tried when one of the partners feels that they can't get their own way through more straightforward means, either because they are the weaker partner, or because their demands are unreasonable.

Women often dominate—and frequently destroy their marriages—by basing every action on the degree to which it is "best for the children." A marriage that was relaxed and companionable with plenty of time and money for an occasional dinner out, a few weekend excursions, and a hobby or two for each, suddenly turns into a desperate affair where all its resources are directed toward catering to the needs of children who must have the best of everything, which only their mother can decide.

Of course, what the children may end up getting is the best of their father on alternate weekends, and the best child-care center while their mother goes to work.

Not only children are used in this way: I know of one woman who showed Dalmations, and used the needs of the dogs to set priorities. Other possibilities are the garden, the decor of the house, illness, what an analyst said, or the demands of a parent.

Housewives naturally play this game using some aspect of their domestic domain as the pretext. Men, on the other hand, typically invoke work or some aspect of finances. For instance, the needs of a man's career provide the pretext for moving, even when the woman has a perfectly good job where they live now, and is in graduate school. They also allow him to demand support services from his wife that he does not, nor would ever, reciprocate, as well as the lion's share of the income for clothing, lunches, a new car, and so on down the line. However this game is played, it is always a destructive one, and while it may not destroy the marriage, it will certainly undermine the good feelings which are essential to it.

There are a number of other powertalk strategies which are destructive to marriages. One of the worst strategies, as well as the most effective, is to rule through weakness and subtalk. The person who, when he tries to discuss some change in his relationship has to give it up because his partner collapses in tears, reproaches him or her for being insensitive and uncaring, or retires to a darkened room with a headache or chest pains, will soon be fantasizing about a divorce. Some other disruptive power strategies within a marriage include:

- Misunderstanding what a spouse says so you can do what you want to do.

- Procrastinating simply to weaken a spouse's will or to avoid implementing unilateral decisions.

- Forgetting. Children are masters at this, but it works between spouses as well as a means of opening up discussions or resuming power struggles.

- Trying to hold a spouse to a promise they never made, or made without understanding the implications of.

- Being late.

Powertalking Teams Can Present a Tremendous Challenge to Outsiders

Some marriage partners operate as powertalking teams outside their relationships. This only works within the framework of a long-term, solid love relationship where both parties are peers and deeply concerned about the other's goals.

In times past, when a man was considered for a top executive post, his wife was interviewed by the wife of the chief executive. Her home was visited to see if the candidate lived the "right way," and the wife was evaluated for her abilities to help her husband and serve as an appropriate and tasteful representative of the company. This frequently created a team with both parties contributing to the advancement of the husband's career. In peer marriages, the wife would be responsible for seeing that the family joined the right clubs, that the right people were entertained in a manner that helped advance the husband, and that he retained control of the conversation by setting up his topics.

In addition, a powertalking wife would be able to brag about her husband in a way that he couldn't, drop the names of his powerful friends in the right ears, expand his power center by talking about his other areas of expertise. Her responsibilities also included keeping her husband's subordinates happy (by remembering events, having parties at the house for them, making herself accessible to them), cementing friendships with higher authorities by making friends with their wives, and using a little selective powertalk to diminish her husband's competitors.

Politicians' wives and a few top corporate wives still perform many of these functions. And modern powertalk teams work in many of the same ways to support one another. A husband may lend the authority of his power center to his wife by bringing some of the influential people he knows to parties primarily for her work colleagues. Both parties may help one another maintain conversational control and advertise their power centers, switching roles to adapt to the power center in which they're operating.

A powertalking team can be one of the best approaches for increasing power in areas of your life outside of your marriage—particularly in the area of your career.

Parent Talk and Kid Talk

If you want your children to grow up into confident powertalkers, you must not use such strong powertalk on them that they're terrified of speaking anything but the most submissive subtalk! Even well-meaning parents frequently go wrong by functioning on a power base that's out of date. In other words, they speak to ten-year-olds as though they're four, teens as if they're ten. Successful parenthood means giving up control gracefully, and moving from control of the totality of a child's life to giving guidance and support. Good parents assume a role of steadily diminishing dominance, and trade control for respect.

Even when speaking to an infant, there's good powertalk and bad powertalk. You can't hurt a child if you use straight powertalk and focus on external factors primarily designed to protect the child. You can do irrepairable damage with powertalk that's clumsy, overbearing, dishonest, and manipulative—particularly if you make the child feel as if he or she has no rights, no wisdom, and should be ashamed of not being who you want him or her to be.

Powertalk that violates the bond of loving will rupture the bond of trust on which all human relationships are built. Powertalk like this can mean your child will never trust anyone nor be trustworthy.

Your powertalk with a child should also be based upon a firm belief that there's an inherent wisdom in every person—so that you instinctively help your child develop this and believe in it. Straight powertalk that clearly establishes rules and punishments for the child's protection and development (and which are appropriate to age and maturity) will give your child a sense of solidity and security.

> **BAD PARENT TALK:** *You horrible beast! I never want to see you again. Get out of this room at once! I think you were born without any sense or human decency!*
> **POSITIVE PARENT TALK:** *I told you that if you threw your dinner, you wouldn't be able*

> *to eat with us. Go to your room and eat dinner*
> *there. We'll try eating together again at the*
> *next meal.*

Just as you permit your spouse autonomy in personal areas, you also need to allow your child freedom to be himself or herself. Powertalk should never be used to legislate feelings, personality, dreams, opinions, or other aspects of the individual self.

Your Child Is Not Your Peer!

Just as many parents err on the side of abdicating parental responsibility, you must neither talk subtalk to your child nor try to establish a true peer relationship. You can certainly allow some give and take in which your child can discuss your decisions and even argue. But you must reserve the right to make certain restrictions and rules, with clear penalties that you stick to. Otherwise, you're teaching your child to manipulate you. Any parent who says, "All right, just this time" is in trouble. (When you constantly change the rules by not imposing particular penalities, your children will rightfully become indignant when you do impose them!)

If you haven't been a consistent powertalker with your child and want to change your relationship, you're in for a tumultuous time. You must insist upon consistency, no matter how your child tries to manipulate you. In the end, however, your child will be happier because there's a great deal of new freedom for children within the bounds of rules.

Changing the Power Balance with Your Children

Before you begin to change the power balance, think your relationship through so you have a clear position to present. It will help you be consistent, if you write down the changes you want to make, the rules you want to establish, the penalties for infractions, and the rules you want to revoke. Once you've done this, you can change the way you handle each issue and situation as it arises. This may mean a long-term struggle with battles over every little thing in the beginning, but it will soon get easier, and will be worth it in the end.

It will help to call a conference and present the new situation. If you've been too heavy a powertalker, admit it, explain what you've done, even apologize. (For example, "I think I've been too rough on you. Let me explain why and let's try some new rules . . . ") If you've been too lenient, state clearly that the situation is changing and you intend to follow the rules you establish from now on without exception.

Of course, this discussion won't end the matter. Any child will test you to see if you really mean it. This testing period can try your intentions, and it's important to recognize that it's going to happen. Be prepared to react calmly, without anger but with firm adherence to your new rules for the relationship.

Powertalking Your Relatives

Extended families are often powertalk hot spots. When you marry, both of your families may spring into action to gain control of the new family unit (you, your spouse, and your potential children). When there's a lot of arguing over the wedding plans, you can be sure that the real situation is a knockdown power battle between the two families. When young families drag small children away from their own Christmas tree to *two* holiday feasts at both in-laws, you can assume the couple is subtalking in a power struggle.

The marriage is in danger when each spouse supports his or her family and joins in the tug-of-war. And when one family is rarely visited on major holidays, you can correctly assume that family (and probably the spouse as well) has submitted to the other.

What do you do when the families line up to battle over you and your (prospective) spouse? First of all, discuss the issue completely with your spouse so the two of you are a powertalk unit, and cannot be separated by guilt manipulation, put-downs, and other techniques. Then powertalk your families, taking control over the decisions as a couple. As long as you're concerned about pleasing your families, and let them make your decisions and shape your opinions, you'll be subtalkers at their mercy.

One power tactic is to assign roles to each member of the family, which gives them a subordinate function, and fails to recognize them as individuals. It's terribly hard to change your position within such a family. Cousin Tim may win the Nobel Prize, but the family will say, "Isn't that nice! Cousin Timmy always was clever with his hands except for that time he took the car apart and couldn't put it back together again."

Even trying to change your name meets with resistance within this type of family. You'll probably be greeted with huffy sarcasm: "Sister wants to be called Marion now! Getting a little too big for your britches, aren't you, dear? Just because you've got some sort of job, you think you're too good for those of us back home?"

At times, you may feel you must battle for power in your family, but it won't be easy because family members will join together against you. The best approach is to line up some allies of your own within the family (and be sure they won't cave in on you at a crucial time), and divide up the family to tackle members alone. Tackle the most powerful one first; his or her submission will often cause everyone else to follow without any further effort on your part. Follow the same tactics you do with a loved one. Get the family member to recognize your ability to use powertalk, and the validity of your power center. Try reasonable discussion (although it rarely works here) and then choose a good time and topic for a full-scale struggle.

Summary

When changing power balances with loved ones, the most important point to remember is that the power struggle should not endanger the life of the relationship. Avoid extremely strong powertalk, power struggles centered upon very sensitive topics. Whenever possible, change the power balance through straight powertalk rather than power games.

If you want to be recognized as a powertalker and you haven't been before, you may have to force your friend or lover to see you in a new light by creating situations in which the other is forced to recognize that you are now a person with power. It's important in these relationships to never speak subtalk again!

If you want to change a relationship that has been based upon negative peertalk, your only option may be to establish a dominant/subordinate relationship since your friend or loved one may be unable to become a powertalker.

Love relationships are often power struggles in which the more committed person has less power than the pursuer. As a relationship moves into long-term commitment, it's very important for the future of the relationship that both parties allow one another power centers and areas of personal freedom within the relationship.

POWERTALK IN BUSINESS

12

Every business has a power hierarchy, a human pyramid with many people on the bottom, fewer as you rise up, and one on top. Ascending the pyramid can only be done at the expense of others. This is the reality of competition, and if you have not yet accepted it, do it now. You can't rise in business if you are not willing to compete.

People who never get anyplace console themselves with the fantasy that jobs open up gradually; if they just do their work and keep their noses clean, they will gradually move into them. This is true only to a small extent. You will, of course, get promoted from time to time if you play it this way, but not very fast or very far. Top management spots the people they want to promote into real power positions long before promotion time, and they manipulate jobs and assignments so that these people move seemingly naturally into the spots where they are needed. So if you are moving far more slowly than you want to be, and more slowly than others in your company, don't blame it on luck.

How well you do your job is often not nearly as important as how well you are perceived to be doing it by upper
management. Merely competent work often goes completely unnoticed, while even outstanding work can easily go under rewarded if you don't play the rest of the
game right. There are numerous examples of leaders in
industry who are not (and never were) particularly effective in their jobs. Instead, they're masters of powertalk,
corporate politics, image building, and ultimately empire
building. This is so much the case, that I think powertalk
should be given equal importance to your work duties,
and sometimes even priority.

How to Be
Viewed as a Potential Leader

In order to rise swiftly, you need to be seen as someone
who will fit in with the leadership. Top officers of a business are very much like members of a private club; they
only open their doors to those who they feel dress right,
have the right tastes and interests, and generally speak
and act right. Right, of course, means like them. You have
to convince these leaders that you are the right kind of
person. But you have to do this somewhat passively. You
can't be seen as trying to muscle into the inner circle
before you are invited. This means avoiding anything
that might seem pushy, overconfident, or assuming a role
that isn't rightfully yours. You have to use the powertalk
style in a way that makes them want you on the team.

It's a bit of a tightrope. If you behave and speak too
submissively, you'll be seen as a subordinate type, and
the judgment will depress your whole career. On the
other hand, if you speak assertive powertalk with your
superiors, and compete with them in dress, accessories,

and the like, you are in danger of being perceived as pushy and overambitious.

The winning strategy is to use positive peertalk with your superiors, and avoid subtalk completely, but to shun all powertalk games and power struggles with them. Let them observe you as a skillful powertalker when you function on their behalf, but be a tactful diplomat when you are in contact with them. Behave graciously with the deference a young person shows to an older one, when they are both of similar class and background and will someday be peers.

Some other helpful hints include: Don't be effusive; don't ask for favors; always pay your own way. Also try to avoid those group get-togethers, which are primarily a reward for subordinates. And if you go, contrive to have it look like an appearance for the sake of democracy. A good approach is to arrive immaculately dressed with an attractive date, stay for an hour, be extremely friendly, and then rush off to make your affair at some elegant club.

Try to join the same clubs as your superiors, and play tennis or golf at the same places. If you are invited to lunch or to the home of a superior, reciprocate within your own means. Take them out to lunch at a place which is less expensive but features unique cuisine. If you receive a gift, return the gesture with a less substantial but well-thought-out present that shows some knowledge of what your employer would like. Keep your business relationship with them efficient and direct, but also try to build a relationship around areas of mutual interest; sports, politics, music, and so on. Do not, however, try to build a relationship around personal issues, and particularly not around personal problems.

It is inappropriate for you to ask a business superior personal questions, and if he asks them of you, it is a way of his establishing his superiority. Should your superior ask personal questions, or volunteer personal advice, respond in a very restrained way, without sounding offended. Asymmetrical personal relationships are one of the primary hallmarks of dominant/submissive relationships.

If you have strengths in areas that have status in the business world, which are neither personal, nor does your superior fancy himself an expert in, you can use these to your advantage. It is acceptable and will gain you points to recommend an excellent wine at dinner, or help your boss refine his golf stroke, providing that you are scrupulous not to cross the line into personal or business issues.

Be Seen as the Best Person at Your Level

Leaders look out for the person who stands out as the leader among his or her peers. This is so important that if you are in an office with someone who is so outstanding you feel you can't compete with them, you might do best to get yourself transferred to another area where you can shine. This is particularly true for women who are working with or under men who assume the credit for everything they do.

On the other hand, if you are not a charismatic type and don't feel you want to try to become one, attach yourself to someone who is, so that you can move upwards together. Don't do this as someone's assistant, if you can avoid it. Instead try to establish some sort of team relationship.

One man I knew was superb at details, and had excellent business judgment, but he was simply uncomfortable with people and the politics that are necessary to rise to top managerial positions. So instead of fighting it, he developed a close working relationship with a man who was very extroverted and a born leader, but had no taste for detail work. Together they made an unbeatable team and rose to a position of great corporate power.

While you are fighting to be a leader, avoid doing anything that could earn you the label of ruthless. No one wants someone like that as a peer, for obvious reasons. Constantly use positive peertalk, and strive to take over as many leadership responsibilities as possible. Never demand others to be subordinate to you; just assume command whenever possible, and you will soon start to be considered a natural leader.

Powertalk from the Driver's Seat

Powertalk is not just for situations where you need more power than you already have. It's also for those situations where you have the power, but the problem is how to get the most out of those who work for you. Next, we are going to look at a common business situation, running a meeting to direct and motivate people.

Why do you need to be skillful in the use of powertalk, when you already have the power? Simple. People in subordinate positions are hardly powerless. They can be cooperative, resourceful, and enthusiastic, or they can be negative, create problems, and totally sabotage your plans—all without ever being insubordinate in any way that you can clearly identify and combat.

Power—by its very nature—creates resentment and negativity among the powerless. And it takes a skillful powertalker to wield power effectively, neither giving up part of it nor using it in such a way as to create a negative backlash.

Calling a Meeting
There are all sorts of reasons for calling a meeting. Most meetings are really a waste of time, but there are a

few that—if handled right—can make a real contribution to getting things done. One of these is the motivational session. This is a meeting you call when you have decided that you want something done in a certain way, and you want to inspire your team to do it that way.

Before you try to run a motivational session, you should know just what you want to accomplish in it. These meetings are managerial tools—not creative tools like brain-storming sessions. Brain-storming sessions generate multiple viewpoints and diversity. Never try to motivate and direct people in the same meeting in which you carry out brain-storming. In a motivational meeting your purpose is just to convert people to your way of thinking, and charge them up to carry out your plans.

Make Them Think Your Idea Is Their Idea ___

Now we come to something of a contradiction. Although you don't want a motivational meeting to become a brain-storming session, it is important to give the illusion that it is one. Nothing motivates people so much as their own ideas. If people always experience themselves just carrying out company policy, they become demoralized and negative. If they feel they are participating in the planning and problem-solving processes, they put much more of themselves into their work. Unfortunately, it is not always practical or wise to get too many people involved in the planning and problem-solving processes. When it is not, you have to look to the next best thing. Get them to feel that the ideas they are facilitating are their own.

Just how do you do this? Surprisingly enough, the first step is to encourage them to express their own thoughts on the subject. And the second step is to recognize and praise the virtues of their ideas.

At this point, you have accomplished two things. You have found out where everyone stands, which gives you the information necessary to best direct the meeting. And you have made everyone feel recognized and valued. The next step is to affirm all those ideas which are in accord with your plans, and to point out those ideas which you don't want to use. Convince others that, despite being brilliant contributions, they are counterproductive for the purposes you have in mind.

While you pretend to analyze the remaining difficulties regarding the ideas of others, you will actually be able to prompt the group into suggesting exactly the things you have already decided to do. There are many ways to accomplish this. One simple approach is to state the problem, wondering out loud how to solve it. As you do this, the group, unless you have them impossibly cowed, will start to volunteer suggestions. Accept and praise each of these suggestions gratefully, but reject them simply by indicating that you are still open for more ideas on the same subject. Sooner or later the group will come up with just what you want them to suggest. When they do, accept these ideas without rejecting the others. Simply say: "Great. That's even better. It's the best idea we've had yet. I think we should start out by trying that one."

If the group doesn't come up with something that you want, think of it yourself. You don't have to tell anyone you came in with the idea. For example: "That's an interesting approach, but I don't think they would go for it upstairs. But it gives me a great idea . . . what do you think would happen if . . ."

They know you're the boss, and, of course, they'll agree. Meanwhile, you've used their ideas and involved them in the planning process. They'll be behind you 100 percent.

Avoid Factional Conflicts _____

It is disastrous to go into a motivational meeting when you are likely to be challenged by a peer or another faction in the company. This stimulates diversity of viewpoint. When people become emotionally committed to ideas, they have a tendency to sabotage other ideas just to prove they were right. Also, allowing yourself to be challenged in a meeting undermines your authority, and suggests to those on your team that they can challenge you as well. If you are likely to meet potential challenges from other areas of roughly equal authority, take care of this first (and privately, if possible). When you present yourself to your team, start out in control.

Acknowledge Everyone's Concerns

Whenever a new project gets put into action, the people involved will have a variety of concerns. Some will deal with things they feel need to get accomplished, like getting more clerical support; others will deal with fears that might arise, like losing authority over an area for which they are responsible.

If these concerns are not quieted, they will spill into other aspects of the decision-making process and undermine the whole meeting. There are ways to quiet these concerns. The most important and—surprisingly—the most frequently overlooked is simply to invite their expression and really listen to them. It is incredible how few managers really take the time to listen to the anxieties of the people on their team, and how reassuring this simple act is.

After you listen to a concern, recognize it. You can do this as simply as just rephrasing it. For example: "I can appreciate your feeling that way, and I will take it into account whatever we decide to do." . . . "Yes, I want you to know I've been aware of that for some time now, and I think it's an important consideration."

The above responses are remarkably noncommittal. All you are saying is that you have heard their concerns, and that you will take them into account. You have not actually promised to do anything, yet it is extremely reassuring. Another response is to indicate you will do something. This can vary from the tentative: "Yes, I am going to put in for more secretarial support in the proposal, although I can't promise we are going to get it" to the more definite: "I understand your fears, and I guarantee that not only will the Johnson account remain yours, but any further accounts of that type will come in your direction." It is important that you do not promise anything specifically, unless you have the capacity to deliver. If you cannot make good on your promises, it will dilute your credibility and lessen your ability to motivate and direct in the future. However, it is usually unnecessary most of the time: Your team will be satisfied if they know that you hear them and are willing to go to bat for them.

Fielding Challenges

Sometimes, in even the best run of meetings, someone will challenge you strongly. When someone does this, it usually means that they have some fear or concern that you have not yet heard. The way to deal with this is to acknowledge their objections, and listen to their alternatives. Then, by questioning them, try to find out what is disturbing them, and offer some kind of solution to their problem. When this procedure doesn't work, you simply have to call rank, although you should try to do it as pleasantly as possible. For example: "I realize that we don't see eye to eye on this one, Bob. I see the appeal of your approach, but all things considered I feel we should go ahead with the procedures I have outlined. If there is anything I can do to facilitate your tasks, I will. In the meanwhile, I expect your wholehearted cooperation."

You should get it, and he should agree graciously. If he doesn't, you have a disciplinary problem on your hands. Deal with it as soon as possible, but not in front of the group. Simply cut him short, and move on with the rest of the agenda. However, at the end of the meeting, pleasantly ask to see him alone. And let the rest of the group hear it. Once alone, try to find out what is wrong, and talk to him about appropriate behavior. But if it continues to be a problem, you will have to fire him.

Summing Up

Now that you have dealt with everyone's concerns, and expressed all your ideas, it is time to go through a process of summing up. This is a very important step. It solidifies the plan and tells everyone what they have decided, and what they are going to do. The summing-up process, if all has gone well, should be similar to what you would have told people to do in the first place. Unless, of course, you happened to get some good ideas in the process, which is always a possibility. The one difference is that in summing up, instead of taking credit for the ideas yourself, you attribute them to various members of the group, or to the group as a whole.

Moving from Consensus to Enthusiasm

If you have gone through all of the above processes, you will have succeeded in creating a good deal of consensus in just what is to be done and how to go about it. Now your task is to build up some extra enthusiasm. Your primary tool for accomplishing this is your own enthusiasm. Talk about what a terrific plan you think it is, how successful you expect to be, how well it is going to be received in the higher echelons of the company, and how everyone is going to benefit from promotions and bonuses if it works out as planned. Finally, let them know how pleased you are with them, and how you expect nothing but the best.

Now you have just a few simple things left to do. First,

you have to assign specific tasks to each person in the group. Give them a time framework in which you expect them to accomplish the work. Finally, arrange a follow-up meeting. This can be done either individually or in a group setting.

Summary

Business power is hierarchical. To attain it, you have to compete successfully and project the right powertalk image.

Corporate leaders only promote those who are adaptable to high-management positions. To fit, you have to sound, look, and act right, which means . . . like them.

To get ahead, speak positive peertalk with your superiors, but neither presume nor push. With your subordinates, speak assertive peertalk, and take command of any projects which could possibly be a source of prestige. Never try to force obedience, and never damage your image by resorting to cutthroat tactics.

If a superior relates to you on a friendly level outside of work, try to create a relationship that is neither related to business nor personal matters. Try to establish mutual interests.

Other points to keep in mind:

- Your overall goal is to be seen as a leader and the best person on your level.

- When running a motivational meeting, start out by knowing what you want. Then try to get people to think your idea is their idea.

- Avoid factional conflicts.

- Acknowledge everyone's concerns.
- Deal firmly with challenges.
- Make sure everyone understands their assignment, and set the date for the next meeting.

POWERTALKING
YOUR WAY INTO
A RAISE AND PROMOTION

13

People are incredibly irrational about asking for a raise. Instead of looking at it as a piece of business strategy, they get their egos involved, taking success as a confirmation of their self-worth and failure as a personal rejection. People have all sorts of misconceived approaches to asking for a raise, but the most common are the following:

1. **Demanding.** Some people feel that getting a raise is a test of manhood (or womanhood); it is a matter of demanding it firmly enough, while having it refused is a form of insult. These are the people who attempt to use powertalk that is too strong. While a demand occasionally works, it is usually because the applicant has an extremely strong position in the company. And when this is the case, very strong powertalk is unnecessary. (I'll say more about this when I talk about the right way to get a raise.) Most of the time, a high-pressure approach is not only unnecessary, but counterproductive.

2. **Ultimatums.** The strongest form of powertalk when asking for a raise is the ultimatum. It is also the worst form in most cases. Even when effective, an ultimatum will make the person receiving it resent you. In fact, some employers will automatically let you go when you give them an ultimatum, even if it is against their own best interests.

3. **Pleas.** The third mistake people usually make when asking for a raise is to plead for it on the grounds of financial need, or even on grounds of fairness. Pleas, on any grounds whatsoever, are subtalk, which puts you in an intentionally weak position. Although pleas occasionally work (you may get a small raise out of pity), they will rarely get you a serious raise. Far worse, pleas will represent you to your employer as an inferior, someone who can be condescended to, and whose gratitude can be purchased for a few crumbs.

The Right Way to Ask for a Raise

The question then arises of just what the right way is to ask for a raise. The answer begins with knowing your value and trading on it. This means not only knowing your value to the firm, but your value in the open market as well. The next question is just how you determine what your value is. There are a number of kinds of value. The first and most important is bottom-line value. Others are irreplaceability, market value, and perceived value. When you ask for a raise on the basis of your value, there are two essential steps to follow:

1. You must arrive at some estimate of what your real

value is. This should be a combination of the four kinds of value discussed above.

2. You must sell your estimate of your value to your employer.

Before you try to determine your value, let's look more closely at the four kinds of value.

Bottom-Line Value

The bottom line of a profitability analysis indicates whether a profit or loss has taken place, and to what degree. Your bottom-line value is simply your contribution to the profitability of your company. Although, in some instances, it may be the degree to which you reduce a loss to your company.

You might have a problem in actually establishing your bottom-line value. There are some types of work, particularly in sales, in which your cash contribution to the company is evident, and you will have no trouble in establishing it. In many areas, however, the relation between the work you do and its contribution to profitability is unclear. Establishing it might take a little creativity. Here are some suggestions:

1. Isolate the area of operations for which you have responsibility. This might be something as elaborate as an entire division or branch, or it might be simply the clerical workers of a given office.

2. Devise some unit by which you can measure your productivity. This can be done in a number of ways, and it will require some ingenuity to figure out how to do it best. Your basic guideline is to figure out what it is that you and the areas under your control do. Then find some common denominator in which to express it.

3. Once you have a way of measuring productivity, it

will be easy to measure your present productivity against that of your predecessors, and build a case for your contribution.

For the head of a secretarial staff, a measure of productivity could be the number of executives whose secretarial requirements are being fulfilled. This can then be weighed against cost in terms of salaries, as well as the cost of any outside services which are necessary. A further measure could be efficiency, in terms of the time taken to get work done.

For an account executive, the measure would be the value of billings, and, of course, any increase in billings, measured against the cost of doing business.

For someone in a creative area, the problem is a little different. Artists, writers, and the like will have to find evidence of improved product performance and customer satisfaction to estimate bottom-line value.

Most businesses have someone who is in charge of financial planning. One of your best bets to determine your productivity is to go to that person (don't reveal that you are trying to build an argument for a raise) and say that you are looking for ways to evaluate your contribution to the company so that you can keep track of it. He or she will help you find the appropriate measures and put together the figures. The following subheadings are intended to give you a basic idea of how to work out your own bottom-line value.

Irreplaceability

Irreplaceability stands right alongside bottom-line value as a measure of how much you are worth to a company. It means that you cannot be removed from your company without serious damage to them. Obviously, if you are irreplaceable, you are in a powerful position, perhaps even the most powerful. And you would tend to think that on the basis of it you can get away with anything, and make the most outlandish demands.

The problem with irreplaceability is that it is a double-edged sword; it works against you as well as for you. Irreplaceable people are extremely threatening to companies just because of the power that they hold. The impulse for any company with an irreplaceable employee is to make them expendable as quickly as possible, and there are many ways to do that: the simplest being to hire you an assistant who will soon learn your job.

Because they are so threatening, irreplaceable people have to bend over backwards to be cooperative and reasonable in every respect. If you are such an employee, you had better make it your business to become the most trusted person in the company. If you do, you will probably get the raises you want just by asking for them, as long as you keep your demands reasonable. If you start throwing your weight around instead, it probably won't be long before someone else appears on the horizon, designated to become irreplaceable in your stead.

If you are irreplaceable, you had better not remind the company of it too often. They will probably be aware of it already. There are, of course, exceptions to this rule. Sometimes a company customarily takes advantage of anyone it can, and you will find that none of your demands have any effect regarding the raise you want. If this is the case, and if you are being hired so cheaply that they are unlikely to be able to replace you for the same salary (even including the raise you are asking for), and if you think they probably have a bit of a guilty conscience, an ultimatum supported by a reminder of your irreplaceability might be in order.

Market Value

Another excellent indication of your worth is your market value. This is what you are worth to other companies in your industry, and it presumes that you have either been offered other jobs, or at least could easily be if you let out the word that you are looking.

Market value is an excellent approach to stating your

worth since it suggests that you could be doing better elsewhere, without actually coming out and threatening or offering an ultimatum. Any employer who hears that your market value is well in excess of what he is paying you, and who really wants to keep you, will probably raise the ante to the degree where he remains competitive. The best way to establish your market value is to solicit offers from other companies; not only is this the surest measure, but it puts you in an excellent negotiating position.

Perceived Value

This refers to what others think you are worth. In a sense, you are always working with perceived value, since that is what the other forms of value all add up to in the end. Here, however, we are talking about the less tangible aspects of perceived value, which come from how well you position yourself in the company politically, and how good an image you present.

If you look and dress right, associate with the power people in your company, manage to get in on the more successful projects, and take credit for the work of those under you, you will probably be perceived as much more valuable than you actually are. We all know smooth operators who are lacking any real talent, but who, due to an excellent image and political skill, function successfully in the realms of management.

The kind of powertalk you use counts for more in establishing your perceived value than almost anything else. In order to be perceived as a leader, it is essential that you always present yourself as a codominant, with just the right amount of deference to your superiors, and as an extremely courteous dominant to your subordinates.

Selling Your Value to Your Boss

Now that you have worked out a measure of your own value to your company, it is time to sell it to your boss as part of the process of attaining a raise. The first step is to set up a time with your boss that is really devoted to you, and where you will be uninterrupted. Tell him or her that you have something important you want to talk about and you would like to set up a meeting to discuss it. Do not tell your boss what it is at the time, and definitely do let him or her talk to you about it at the coffee machine or while walking down the corridors. Demand that time be set aside. If you get started and he begins to rush you or interrupt for calls or other business, tell him that you see he is busy, and you would like to reschedule the meeting for a time when he can give you his complete attention.

Once you have his uninterrupted attention, present the case for your value directly, using polite, codominant powertalk. For example: "Since I arrived in the company, I have increased productivity by Y percent or Z dollars. At the same time, operating costs have gone down by . . . , or only increased by . . . , a savings of . . . Furthermore, I have accomplished such and such and received the following recognition. . ."

At this point, should you be lucky enough to have a fair employer who is also doing sufficiently well to be able to grant your desired raise, his response may well be: "Very well, just how much of an increase are you looking for?"

Always name a figure. Never leave it up to your employer to suggest one. Chances are it will be far below what you had in mind, and it will probably be less than what he would be willing to grant. (People always start out by offering less.) Furthermore, it allows him to set the starting point for the negotiations and puts you in the uncomfortable position of naming a higher raise. If you name the first figure and it is too high (it should be), he is in the equally uncomfortable position of cutting you down. Don't worry about his feelings too much, though; he can take care of himself.

Just decide what you want for the raise—being realistic but not conservative—and then raise it by at least 50 percent. This is to give your boss room to negotiate, and you room to come down, so that you can't be accused of being unreasonable.

Present your demand in your very best powertalk. Avoid all subtalk devices. Do not apologize for yourself, and definitely do not say, "I know it sounds like a lot of money, but I think I'm worth it." Just look him or her in the eyes and say in a matter-of-fact voice, "I'm looking for another twelve thousand." If you give the slightest indication that you are hesitant, uncertain, or think you are asking for too much money, your employer will pick it up instantly and try to knock it down.

Games Employers Play

There is a small chance that your employer will say, "I'll go for eight." Then you can reply, "How about ten?" Perhaps you can both happily settle on ninety-five, but this probably won't happen. It is more likely that your employer will counter with a brilliant array of maneuvers, which he has been perfecting for decades, designed to discourage you from asking for a raise at all, or at worst, knocking you down to a miniscule one. The following are some of the games employers will play, and the basic powertalk strategies you can use to counter them.

TAKING YOU INTO THEIR CONFIDENCE

Beware of the employer who suddenly takes you into his confidence during salary negotiations. It will never be to tell you how well the company is doing; and it will always cost you money. Suddenly, you will be privy to all sorts of confidential information about the problems the business is having with profits, cash flow, the IRS, controlling costs to meet the competition, and so on. The proper way to respond to these confidences is to be interested and sympathetic, but keep it clear that it is not your problem.

If he persists with the above strategy, reply: "I understand that the business is experiencing difficulties, but I have personal financial difficulties of my own. I am not trying to make you responsible for these, and I don't think it is fair to penalize me for the company's problems. I give the company my best effort, and I have a right to be fairly compensated for the contribution I make."

If he continues to push, you might say that you only think it is fair to be penalized by the company's difficulties if you profit equally by its successes. Ask him if he would be willing to discuss some sort of plan which incorporates profit sharing and a bonus system for any savings or increased revenues which you generate. (However, be careful with this approach; some companies are run so that they never show any profit, while the owners and principal shareholders take home extremely handsome salaries and benefits.)

"CRYING POLICY"

Another way in which crafty employers are fond of defeating requests for raises is to "cry policy." The employer grants the validity of your request, and implies he would like to meet it, but says that he cannot because company policy forbids raises of over two percent, raises for people who have been there less than three years, raises above a certain level for people in your job, raises for people with less than 60 percent Indian blood, or whatever other argument he can muster.

There are a number of ways in which you can try to get around a boss who uses this tactic. One that sometimes works is to threaten to go over his head. You say: "I understand you are bound by these policies. Who is the appropriate person with the power to bend these rules?" This is an interesting strategy, which you can only use when there is someone higher up to whom to make your appeal. On the other hand, it is pretty hard for the head of a company to cry policy, because you can always ask him who made the policy. People hate to have you go over their heads; it confirms the unpleasant fact that there is someone in that position; it also takes the entire situation out of their control and brings a superior into the picture. The problem with this approach is that it can create hostility, but sometimes when you are fighting for a raise a little hostility is inevitable. I would caution, however, against ever going over someone's head without their actually clearing it first. The success strategy in this situation is to get your boss to approve a raise for you in principle, when he is feeling secure behind his policy, then go over his head to get the policy changed.

Another approach is to get the boss to discuss the policies with you in detail, and then try to find ways around them, or come up with some reasons why you should be an exception. If the problem with the policy is that it is too early for you to get a raise, you can use this to bargain for a larger raise later.

Frequently, the policy will be stated in terms of the maximum salary that can be paid to someone in your particular job at your level. There are a couple of ways around this. One is to look around the firm for others in comparable jobs who are being paid more than you. Another—and an excellent one—is to use this as an opportunity to bid for promotion. (We'll talk more about how to get a promotion in the next section.)

Forestalling Tactics

Sometimes your boss will try to handle the entire raise problem by forestalling your requests with some action designed to take the wind out of your sails. These are usually moves designed to make it seem that you are being given so much that you feel guilty about demanding anything more.

TOKEN RAISES

One tactic that canny employers use to forestall the demand for a raise when they see it coming is giving you a raise first—one far smaller than they expect you to have in mind. This pittance is offered with elaborate

thanks for your marvelous contributions, with a statement of regret that for various reasons it couldn't have
been twice or even four times as much (which is what you
had in mind in the first place). Your boss will offer hopes
that sometime soon he or she will be able to give you
something closer to what you deserve. Note the suggestion that you will never get all you deserve, so don't
bother asking for it. If you let this last suggestion go
unchallenged, you will be tacitly agreeing to accept an
ongoing pattern of undercompensation.

The only way to handle token raises is to nip them in
the bud, which might be a little tricky if you haven't quite
gotten up your courage to ask for a raise yet, and you are
caught unawares. If you can think quickly enough to do
it, thank your employer profusely, then point out that you
had been about to ask for a raise, but that the token offer
is so low as to be inadequate. Express that you were looking for something more along the lines of . . . and name
your inflated negotiating figure.

If, as is more likely the case, it is not until much later
that you realize how thoroughly put off you have been,
the trick is to get back to him as quickly as possible. Tell
him that you felt a little awkward bringing it up the day
before, but you had been about to ask for a raise. Unfortunately, what he is offering you is far too little; then
proceed as above.

Time is your enemy here. The more time you allow to
elapse after hearing about the token raise, the weaker
your position will be with your employer. Furthermore,
by accepting a token raise, you will be initiating a compensation pattern that will become harder to break,
which might eventually force you to leave the company in
order to get the money you deserve.

PERKS

The other major forestalling tactic employers use is to
reward you with perks instead of raises. This is a trickier
question than the previous one. Sometimes perks will be

more in your favor than the raises will be. This is particularly the case for those who already pay a large tax. If you are in that category, the use of a company car is worth more to you than what the same car would cost you, provided, of course, the company does its books in a way that doesn't leave you having to pay a tax on the car.

Much of the time, however, perks in lieu of salary have to be examined carefully. Many times a company that gives you an assistant will try to use that as an excuse not to pay you a raise. Point out that your assistant is not for your personal use, but to increase your productivity for the company. If they want to provide you with a housekeeper, chauffeur or butler, that would be a different story.

Other perks include things like a larger office or the proverbial keys to the executive washroom. The response to any of these is simply to point out that they are all the more reason for you to expect to be paid on a level with your position.

The important point to remember with perks, as with all forestalling tactics, is that they are meant to make you feel guilty about demanding a raise. Keep this in mind, and refuse to feel guilty. If you can keep clear about your wants, and remain determined to ask for and get compensation, you will have won half the battle. In fact, you can use any form of self-recognition to your advantage by using it to reinforce your claim that you deserve a raise. After all, any company that values you enough to give you an assistant, and a larger office, ought to value you enough to give you a decent raise.

SILENT POWERTALK

You should never threaten or give your employer ultimatums. However, there are times when it is necessary to at least drop a few hints that you are dissatisfied. The basic technique is to create an air of secrecy, with the newspaper folded to the classified section, or quietly working on your resume during your lunch hour. If these do not do the trick, the problem really might be that you are not as highly regarded as you think you should be in your company. Perhaps you should be thinking of moving on in earnest!

The Best Way to Get a Raise Is to Get a Promotion

There are three kinds of promotions:

MOVING UP

Moving up means simply to be promoted to the next higher rank that already exists within your company. The way to be moved up is to do your job well, speak powertalk, stay out of trouble, and make friends wherever they are likely to be of benefit. Compared to other ways of getting promotions, there is relatively little you can do to get yourself moved up.

EXPANDING

The second way to get promoted is through selectively expanding or contracting your present job. Many jobs, especially in smaller companies, have elastic boundaries. For instance, many assistant jobs have a bottom end, which might include filing and calling out for lunch, and a top end, which would embrace executive responsibilities and decision-making powers. The trick in expanding your job is to take on as many higher functions as you can, and delegate all of your lower functions to someone else. It is always important to expand upwards first. That way, if anyone resists your telling the secretary to follow up on the lost hotel reservations, you can point out that you would be glad to do it yourself but, unfortunately, that conflicts with your renegotiating the printing contract.

Once you have sufficiently expanded the top end of your job, and delegated away the bottom, you can go to your immediate employer and say, "Look, I was hired as an executive secretary, and now I'm totally in charge of producing the in-house newsletter, and a lot of PR functions as well. Don't you think it would be fair to promote me into an executive-level position?" When you have the new position, it is easy to come back to your boss and renegotiate salary on the strength of the new position.

CREATING A NEW JOB

The most daring and innovative way of getting a promotion is to create a new job. This is similar to expanding upward, but there are two main differences. Whereas expanding upward means taking on tasks that already exist, creating a new job is a more visionary act that requires seeing the need for something within the company, and then selling a number of people on your idea. Therefore, expanding is a gradual process of development; creating a new job entails a major leap.

Selling your company on the need for a new job is like selling anything: you first have to sell the idea of the need. Point out exactly what the hole or shortcoming in present operations is, and how the job you are proposing can help the overall situation.

For instance, suppose you work as an assistant editor for a company that publishes textbooks. The textbooks are written by different authors, but your company turns them into complete teaching packages, including, among other things, the creation of instructors' manuals written for them.

Previously, each instructor's manual had been put together by the author of the book, with the help of the editor, and had usually been more of an afterthought. Now you have the feeling that a high-quality instructor's manual could be a great selling point for all your texts. It might give your company a real edge in the market, particularly for lower-level institutions where instructors might be more interested in convenience and ease, rather than the particular theoretical orientation a given text has.

Your thought is that a special editorial position should be created just to handle the development of these instructors' manuals, and that this editor's first job should be to survey the field and develop standards for a completely new and superior form of manual, which could then be uniform throughout your company's books.

Let's suppose that you want to create this position, and naturally make sure that it is offered to you. First, you must set forth a detailed presentation, which includes your basic statement of what is lacking and a plan for remedying it. You should also include such aspects as time estimates, costs, advantages, and reasonable expectations of profits.

Furthermore, you should do some real groundwork in developing guidelines for this new instructor's guide, interviewing department heads in various schools and surveying what other publishers are doing. And on the basis of this, you should do some preliminary investigative work on your own—enough to demonstrate that you have a real handle on this field and are the logical choice for the job.

Now you are ready to sell your proposal to the decision makers in your company. Be careful to work within the hierarchy of command, and build support all the way. Begin with your immediate supervisor. Take him to lunch and sell the idea to him. You have to convince him not only that the idea is good for the company, but that it is good for him as well. Give him time to think it over, but continue selling the idea until he buys it. Your plan is to form a team with him, so that the two of you are behind the project.

Next you are ready to go up the line. This is tricky; you can do it alone or with your immediate supervisor, but it is important to get his backing first. Once you have this backing, you can say, "Where do you think I should go with this now?" Or "I think it's probably time to show this to Joe Morello. How do you think we should go about it?"

At this point, he will let you know if he wants to go with

you, or whether he is happy to let you proceed alone. It depends on two things: how decent a person he is, and what he thinks of the project. If he is excited about the project and wants to share the glory, he will want to come along for the ride. On the other hand, if he is a little hesitant about it, he might stay right behind you, and see how you fare before he commits himself. Whichever is most desirable depends both on him and the project. If you think he might want to take it away from you, try to leave him behind as much as possible. On the other hand, if he is well placed and secure, and you think he only wants a little glory, his presence and support will be invaluable.

Once you get the support of the next person up the line, it becomes a matter of snowballing, getting more and more people involved until you have a major proposal, with your name on it.

Should you manage to pull this off, you will be the only logical person to take the job (unless you are unrealistic enough to promote a position for which you are hopelessly unqualified). And with the new position, it will be easy to ask for a raise. Even if you don't succeed, you will have made a great many people aware that you are there and have more than the usual degree of talent and ambition—and that can't hurt.

Really Getting the Promotion _____

There are a couple of games employers are fond of playing with promotions, and you should be aware of them. Your boss may be giving you the promotion without a suitable salary raise, a higher title, or without relieving you of the work you were responsible for before the change.

NO RAISE

The way to deal with this one is through direct—though never impolite—confrontation. If you ask for a raise that is commensurate with your new position, it will be up to your employer to provide reasons why he is with-holding it. Then you can deal with these according to the guidelines in the first part of this chapter. A lame but surprisingly common employer's response is to say you just got a promotion, and that the raise will come in time, with a caution for you not to be greedy. Your response should simply be to insist that a promotion is not really a promotion without a raise; it is just giving you more work without a reward.

NO TITLE

This is sometimes done when a change in your title will force your company to make other changes, which for a variety of reasons, they might be reluctant to do (for example, paying you a lot more money, having you report to someone higher up than your present boss, or promot-ing you over someone else's head). Title is extremely important, and you have to fight for it. But sometimes you are better off taking one thing at a time. If you get an effective promotion, and particularly if you get a raise, it might be wise to stay with the new job until you have a track record. Then you can come back and say, "Look, I've been doing the work of a supervisor for three months now, and I'm still being called a trainee. Isn't it about time this promotion was made official?"

NO RELIEF

Do you want that promotion so badly you are willing to do the job of two people instead of one? That might be just what your boss is banking on when he gives you a new title, lots of extra responsibilities, and a modest raise, without hiring someone else to take on your old job. This happens frequently, and it is a tricky situation to handle. Here is one possible scenario:

You have been moved from a secretarial position to what is presumably an executive one: assistant to the sales manager. By some coincidence, this is just the person you were secretary to previously, and it just so happens he has not hired another secretary. You now have a great mass of new work, and all of your old work as well. After about three weeks of working lunches and overtime, you hit on a strategy. You'll do all the higher-level work but leave the typing and filing undone. Four days later, your furious boss is complaining that you are not keeping up with your work.

> BOSS: *What's going on here, Janet? I've just given you a major promotion, and now you're neglecting your work, and the whole office is backed up.*
>
> JANET: *That's untrue. I'm not neglecting my work. All my administrative functions have been carried out. Furthermore, I'm ahead of schedule on developing the Ferguson report.*
>
> BOSS: *Yes, but what about that pile of typing and filing on your desk?*
>
> JANET: *That's all clerical work—not my work. I was promoted to an administrative assistant, remember?*
>
> BOSS: *Yes, but the idea was for you to grow into new areas of responsibility—not to give up doing all the things you are good at.*
>
> JANET: *I am growing into new areas, and very quickly. I didn't mind helping with the clerical work, while you looked for a new secretary and I had time. But I've been getting busier and busier with my real work.*
>
> BOSS: *Maybe this promotion was premature, and your new responsibilities are too much to handle.*
>
> JANET: *That's completely untrue. The problem is that there is an enormous amount of administrative work that I'm taking over, and I feel I'm doing a good job with it. I was*

doing the work of two secretaries before, now I'm doing the work of two administrators. I can't do the work of four people. The truth is you just need a secretary, and frankly, I'll be needing some secretarial help myself before long.

COMMENTARY

The boss's goal is to get Janet to take over some of the less gratifying administrative tasks he was saddled with, and to keep her doing the secretarial work as well. He thought he could accomplish that by the simple task of giving her a promotion (in title) and a modest raise. It would be far cheaper than hiring a second person. He was counting on Janet being so grateful for the promotion that she would overwork herself to make good.

Janet's goal, on the other hand, is to make the promotion into a real promotion, not just a glorified secretarial position. Her basic strategy for doing this is the same as the strategy for getting a promotion by expanding your job on the upper end, and contracting it on the lower end. Her biggest problem is dealing with the demands of a frustrated and irate boss, who is not getting the grateful slave he counted on, but rather a feisty junior executive. He is, of course, trying to pressure her with guilt into meeting his expectations and she is using powertalk to resist him. Her boss is not done yet, however. He has a few more tricks up his sleeve.

BOSS: *Okay, if you're really that busy, give me back some of the administrative work, and I'll help you catch up. But get that pile of typing off your desk.*

COMMENTARY

This is a difficult play to counter. Janet can't very well give her boss the filing, and he is counting on her not wanting to give up the administrative work. She has two options. She could make a stand and refuse to do any clerical work. However, this requires a real confrontation, which could be disastrous. Another possibility would be for her to load up her boss with so much work that there is no way he would be willing to do it. Then he would be more motivated to see the merits of her position.

Unfortunately, the boss has an answer to this, and a very effective one at that. He can accept the work, but not do it, waiting for some pretext like a sudden business trip, and dump it back into her lap days before the deadline for its completion.

The assistant's only possible recourse is to quit or do the work, but she can make it very expensive in terms of other things that do not get done. Perhaps her best strategy is to do it, while claiming that the only way she can get it done is to get a temporary worker to do the typing. This sets the stage for the hiring of another secretary, which is her ultimate goal.

There are some other strategies the boss can try. He can be condescending and vaguely threatening. He can say, "Listen, Janet, you are an executive now. Executives don't punch a time clock like secretaries. They just work until their work is done." Or he can hold out the promise of a reward. "It would be wonderful if no one had to do any routine work, but unfortunately we all have our share. Why don't you just put your back into it for a while? In six months or so we will see about getting you some assistance if it still seems necessary."

Obviously, Janet can field each of these maneuvers with assertive powertalk. In fact, she might be forced to do it, but the problem is that this tends to develop an excessively confrontational atmosphere. A far better approach for her would be to try to renegotiate and redefine the entire situation. She needs to call a meeting with her boss and discuss the entire issue.

Her goal in this meeting is to come to an agreed-upon

definition of her job—one that protects her promotion and gives her a fair break, but still ends the escalating conflict with her boss. She wants to get rid of as much lower-level work as possible and trade it for upper-level work. Once her boss puts her job description in writing, there will be a basis for discussion. If the job is clearly unfair, including everything from getting coffee to being in charge of sales, she will have an easier time arguing that she needs to be relieved of the less skilled duties. At any rate, the job description must never be accepted as it is offered, but used as a basis for negotiations with the goal of divesting herself of as many clerical duties as possible.

Once she takes this negotiating process as far as she can, it is still very likely that she will be left with more clerical and menial duties than she would like. In this case, she has to agree to try and complete the work, pointing out that obviously there will be times when there will be more than she can do. Then she must ask for priorities to be set so that she knows what to do first. She also should try to establish an operating procedure for those times when everything can't be finished, making it necessary to bring in a temporary worker. Her goal is to build a case for hiring another full-time secretary. If she is successful with this overall negotiation strategy, she should be able to protect her promotion, and eventually get exactly what she wants, even though she will have to compromise a little at the outset.

Summary

Ultimatums are both the strongest and the worst way to ask for a raise, because they create resentment. Pleas, coming from a point of weakness, are subtalk, and also a weak way to proceed. The right way to ask for a raise is to establish your value for the company, and then trade on it.

There are four kinds of value: bottom-line, irreplaceability, market value, and perceived value. Once you establish your value, you must sell it to your boss.

You must learn to counter the games employers play. The best way to get a raise is to get a promotion. This can be done by moving up, expanding, or creating a new job. There are also a number of ways employers tend to cheat you out of your promotion, such as withholding raises or holding you responsible for your old work. You must learn to counter these tactics by powertalking your way to a more satisfactory agreement.

POWERTALK
SALESMANSHIP

14

The point of all salesmanship is to make your client want to buy what you have to sell more than he doesn't want to spend the money for it (and, of course, more than he wants to buy what your competitors are selling). There are entire libraries on salesmanship, and I can't possibly cover the whole subject here. Rather, I want to concentrate on how powertalk makes the greatest contribution, which is in establishing the right *image relationship* between yourself and your client.

Image relationship refers to the image of yourself and your product that you choose to project to a client, taking into account not only his business needs, but his personal needs as well.

For example, some buyers may need to feel that the people they buy from are personal friends who would never deal unethically with them. Others look for people they can get great bargains from, while still others look for experts who will give them free advice along with the products. The salesman who is alert to these nuances, and tailors the image he presents accordingly, will be able to develop loyalty from a great variety of clients.

Whenever you sell something, you are selling yourself as well. To be a really effective salesman, you have to establish certain fundamental qualities in your relationship with your client: most basic of these is trust. If your client doesn't trust you as a person, he or she will discount your statements, and consequently be extremely sales resistant. Along with trust, you must create the right image relationship with your client. Assuming your product is appropriate to your customer's needs and competitive, your image relationship is the largest single factor in getting and keeping your customers.

The Ethical Image

Whatever the personal makeup of your client, it is imperative that you project an ethical image to him. There are two types of ethical image:

1. **Product ethics.** This is a matter of offering a bona fide product or service, which is of high quality, accurately represented, and responsibly backed. This, however, is where your responsibility ends. You do not take responsibility for the purchaser, and guarantee him that your product or service is the best solution for his needs.

2. **Client ethics.** This implies that your ethics cover not only your product but your relationship to your client. You must honestly help him to evaluate his business, and recommend the best products and services to him—even to the point of sending him to another company if you cannot meet his needs.

Product ethics are sufficient for people who are selling in stores, where they give the customer the facts and leave it up to him to decide whether he wants the product. However, this service is insufficient for most business sales. In business, you are not only a salesman but a consultant, and it is not enough just to offer a product; you must offer direction as well. If you can convince a client of your ability to do this, he will most likely be your client forever (once again, assuming that you continue to represent an appropriate, high-quality, and competitive product).

There are, of course, numerous ways of projecting a competitive image, but the simplest and most effective way is to be ethical. People are remarkably sensitive to the most subtle indications of honesty. Furthermore, they frequently test the honesty of sales reps before they buy. If they catch you bending the facts, they will become distrustful and resistant. After that, you won't even be able to interest them in a bargain.

One common test that smart buyers employ is to ask the salesman naive questions about competing products, when you already know the answer. If the salesman lies, he will lose credibility, but even claiming ignorance will work against him. A good sales rep should be familiar with the competition, in order to best represent his client. Of course, he is still going to try to sell his product, but he must do it by showing its real advantages over the competition, not by disparaging the competition.

The best response to this sort of "naive" query is to enter into a frank discussion of the merits of the two products, as if you were the customer's business associate or friend. Let him tell you what his doubts are about the competition. Remember that he probably has them; otherwise, he probably would have bought already.

Another important aspect of ethical image is to appear to come from a position of strength, not neediness. If the customer perceives you as anxious to make a sale, he will naturally suspect you. This is why smart salesmen usually try to give the impression that business is great, and their main problem is in keeping up with orders.

There is one strategy in which it is advantageous to

give the impression of coming from weakness. This is when you are trying to convince the customer that he is getting a bargain. If he thinks you are virtually helpless, and that he is taking advantage of you, it won't occur to him to distrust you. (We will talk more about this strategy when we look at selling from a subordinate position.)

High-Pressure Tactics

Although you might think that a chapter on selling through powertalk would be mostly about high-pressure tactics, the opposite is true. Pressure tactics are tricky; they interfere with trust and easily backfire. Usually they are most effective with the least sophisticated customers, and put off more experienced ones.

There are a couple of mild pressure tactics which you might want to try. The most effective of these is simple enthusiasm. This is really not pressure so much as just energy, but it is amazing how far it will get you. The trick is to develop and convey a real enthusiasm for what you are selling, with the conviction that it will really do the job better than the competition. Real enthusiasm will carry the prospective customer along, convince him of your credibility, and make him want to buy.

The other tactics you might want to try have to do with finalizing the deal. The following are some of them:

Closing Tactics

Try not to ask the prospective customer if he is ready to buy if you can help it. This makes it too easy for him to say no. Instead, assume he is buying. One way to do this is to begin writing the order and then ask him some question: "Do you want brown or blue?"

Another ploy is to start working on prices and delivery times. "Let's see what that would really cost you." Or "Before we go any further, let me check the warehouse and see if I can really deliver." Once you have gotten this far, it is easy to throw in a clincher: "Do you want to take all twelve now? If you do, I can get you a 15 percent volume discount." Or "What luck, there is a special sale price in effect until Friday. That'll save you . . . let's see . . ." or "They're completely backed up, but they have one cancellation. If you want to take it now, I can get it for you immediately, otherwise, you'll have to wait at least nine weeks. What'll I tell them?"

If the customer feels rushed and balks, you can offer him an out: "You can always return it for a full refund." Or "Why don't you order it now so you don't miss your chance? If you reconsider, just call me anytime in the next twenty-four hours. I've got at least three other customers who'll jump at the chance to take it."

Image Relationship Approaches

The concept of the image relationship suggests you evaluate each client's personal and business needs and then take an approach that best fits them. The following are the fundamental approaches you have to choose from, with some guidelines on which types of clients need which ones:

THE PEER APPROACH

When you have a mature client who intelligently seeks to buy a product or service in order to fill a real business need, the best way to approach him is as a peer. Talk positive peertalk, be friendly and reasonably deferential, but never compromise your codominance.

To a certain extent, you may enter into your client's decision process in that you can tell him how your products and services can bring him efficiencies of operation or higher profits, but be careful about telling him how to run his own business. Your assumption is that you are the expert in your business and he is in his.

The relationship between buyer and seller is an extremely emotional one; many customers, including many highly placed executives and professionals, do not want a peer approach. Sometimes they even want someone to tell them what to do.

THE AUTHORITARIAN APPROACH

Some buyers are extremely uncertain, not only about what to buy, but even about what their real needs are. These people frequently seek a salesman who is not only authoritative but tells them what to do.

Buyers who want to be approached like this will clue you in by the questions they ask and the information they offer about their needs. They will tell you far too much about their business and its problems or (if it is a personal purchase) about their personal life. Then they will ask your advice about things which seem to go far beyond what is appropriate to your role as a sales rep.

The best way to speak to a client like this is to use assertive powertalk when telling him what to buy, combined with a warm, almost parental, personal approach. Act as if the customer is your son or daughter, and sternly but caringly tell him or her what to do for their own good.

THE CONSPIRATORIAL APPROACH

Another type of customer will want you to enter into a conspiratorial relationship with him. Like the previous client, he will tell you an inappropriate amount about his needs and what he is planning to use your products or services for. But unlike the previous type of customer, he will not ask for advice. He is looking for agreement and support and a coconspirator in his plans.

Talk positive peertalk with this client. Be agreeable and informal, match his enthusiasm and pick up his clues. You don't have to do much with a customer like this; he is going to sell himself if he is going to buy at all.

All he wants you to do is share his enthusiasms and fantasies. Do it, and you will make a loyal customer.

THE VICTIM APPROACH

An approach that is demeaning, but which nevertheless is the most effective one for certain kinds of customers, is the victim approach. Some people will only buy when they feel they have the upper hand. They look for a salesman who is in a difficult position, and due to financial problems, heavy competition, or the like must make a sale, even at the cost of cutting profits, tacking on free extras, and taking a certain amount of personal mistreatment. The victim approach is a staple in discount outlets and ghetto stores where bargain hunting is the norm. These merchants play the victim outrageously, plastering their windows with lost-lease signs, confiding to their customers that they are giving away merchandise below cost, and so on. But the game exists on all levels of the economy. The only people who must never play this game are professionals who must always appear to be successful.

Of course, the salesmen who play this game are seldom really victims. They incorporate healthy markups into their price structures, and even when they cut prices they have comfortable profits.

Victim salesmen talk a unique mixture of powertalk and subtalk. Subtalk is their basic style, as they defer to their customers' wishes and go out of their way to please. However, they mix it with a very intrusive form of powertalk when the customer either resists the sale or bargains too hard. The overall strategy is to convince the customer that he is getting an incredible deal, and that the salesman is going to lose his shirt and be grateful as well. However, should the customer fail to cooperate, either by expressing doubts or pushing the bargain too far, the salesman will turn threatening, and imply that he is now being taken advantage of; if it doesn't stop, he is going to refuse to continue to sell to that customer.

Tailor Your Language to Your Product _____

Another consideration that should affect your powertalk style is the product you are selling, and what it is you are selling about it!

What do I mean by this? Let's say, for instance, that you are selling a car. You don't sell the whole car at once; you sell different aspects of it: the style, the performance, the economy. Furthermore, you sell the different aspects in succession, gradually building an effect on the customer. As you proceed, your powertalk style changes so that it is always in keeping with the subject. If you begin with style, you should start with a language that is conspiratorial, appreciative, even extravagant: "Look at those curves" and "What a honey!" Then you might proceed to performance or construction and get authoritative and technical: "Of course, there is no comparing the two suspension systems; the one has fully independent suspension on all four wheels, and the other works with two solid axles. Its design hasn't changed in forty years." Then you play the victim when you talk price, and finally when it comes to service, you speak a dignified, ethical, positive peertalk, reassuring your customer that you will always be there to back up this great car you are letting him steal from you.

Finally, at the close, you become very businesslike, and matter of fact. Start writing up the order before you even close the deal, letting it be known that you consider the matter settled, and you expect him to sign on the bottom line with no more discussion.

Speak Your Clients' Language _____

The last consideration to influence your powertalk selling style should be your clients' language. The way in which he speaks offers invaluable clues about who he is and what the best way is to respond to him.

For instance, if he uses technical language, it is a sign that he is either well informed and scientifically minded, or at least wants to be seen that way. If you respond with your typical routine targeted at uninformed customers, you will irritate and insult him. He wants to be spoken to on a technical level, which presupposes he is your peer or equal—not only in general intelligence, but in the background necessary to understand your particular product.

If, on the other hand, he presents himself intelligently, making no attempt to speak the language of the product, and asks basic questions, your task is to speak to him in nonspecialized language. Do not condescend to him in any way.

If he seems extremely compulsive and anxious—worried about every little detail and comparing your product to all others in every possible way—he basically is a type that needs to feel that he has covered the bases and made the right choice. Be patient. Go through the whole process with him, pointing out the superiority of your product at each turn, helping him to overcome his objections.

If he asks a lot of questions about price and value, talk price and value at length with him. If your price is higher than the competition, you must break it down and show him how due to extra features or longevity he ends up getting more value for his money. If you are not successful in doing this, you will lose the sale, even though he might emotionally prefer your product. This is particularly important for people who sell things like cars where style and image are important. Some people will want to buy your products, but will end up purchasing the biggest bargains. If you can convince them that your product is the better value, even though more expensive, you can convert many of these wishful excursions into real sales.

Men Selling to Women

Many salesmen, who are naturally adept at finding the right approach when selling to men, completely fail when they try to sell to women. The problem has—if anything—gotten trickier in this era of changing sex roles.

Once, the salesman selling to women only had to choose between two approaches, the sexist-paternalistic approach for women his age or younger, or the nice boy approach for older women. The waters have been considerably muddied by the emancipation of the older woman. This kind of woman expects to be treated as a peer, and is on guard for anything that smacks of sexism. The question for the salesman is how to decide which approach is appropriate for which customer. The answer is to let the customers tell you by the manner in which they approach you.

THE SEXIST-PATERNALISTIC APPROACH

This is the old standby: superior, condescending, and replete with sexual innuendo, which used to be the accepted way men related to women, but which women are increasingly objecting to nowadays. What is confusing is that along with the great numbers of "new women" who will take severe offense if you relate to them in this way, there remain great numbers of traditional women who will take offense if you do not.

Women who prefer a traditional approach will usually approach you somewhat coquettishly. They will make a lot of eye contact, and often somewhat intimate remarks or jokes, as if the relationship were personal and not business. They will discuss the product nonassertively, putting their trust in you and soliciting your opinion.

If you are an older man selling to a much younger traditional woman, the flirtatious element in the way you relate to her should give way to something much more paternal. Your style should be that of a disinterested gentleman guiding a young woman through the intricacies of buying your product, with just a suggestion that were you but twenty years younger you would be interested in her.

THE NICE BOY APPROACH

Many women, when they reach a certain age or position, give up their girlish self-image and adopt a matronly image instead. A matron is a middle-aged (or older) woman whose self-worth derives from her responsibilities, accomplishments, and position in life.

Matronly women frequently reject the sexist-paternalistic approach and demand the nice boy approach instead. The essence of this is the image of a well-bred, obedient young man who is humble, ambitious, and eager to please. The archetype is the junior bank clerk in turn-of-the-century, small-town America, waiting on the judge's wife. However, you don't have to be young and unaccomplished for the nice boy approach to be demanded of you. A really determined matron might as easily demand it of her stockbroker or her fifty-year-old internist. As matrons become elderly, they tend to see all men younger than themselves as either ill-bred boys who don't cater to them, or nice ones who do.

A women who wants the nice boy approach will cue you by treating you like one. She will be demanding, condescending, and officious, and tend toward a no-nonsense tone of voice. If you miss your cue and respond with the sexist-paternalistic approach, it is possible that she might accept it and switch to a softer, more coquettish style. What is more likely is that she will simply correct you; she is unlikely to get seriously offended. If, however, you refuse to relate to her in either way, but rather stand on your dignity and relate appropriately and professionally, resisting her attempts to reduce you to a boy, you will redefine yourself in her mind from being a nice boy to a fresh kid. You can rest assured that she will complain to your superior if you don't give her satisfaction. If you have no superior, she will take her business elsewhere.

THE EQUAL APPROACH

More and more contemporary women are demanding to be treated as equals by men. They do not want to be talked down to, treated lightly, or have their specific questions dismissed with vague reassurances. In particular, they do not want to be related to as potential sex objects.

The woman who wishes to be treated like an equal will usually approach you in a matter-of-fact way, which might range from formal and reserved to casual and friendly. It is easy to mistake the friendly approach of a liberated woman as a flirtatious one. If you make this mistake and switch into the sexist-paternalistic approach, she will soon correct your error.

It is sometimes a little tricky to sell things requiring technical expertise to liberated women, at least those who are lacking in technical background without sounding condescending. This is because it is hard to talk about technical matters nontechnically. The trick is to explain things thoroughly and carefully, and avoid using jargon. Do it the same way you would explain something for a man whose background might be limited, but whose intelligence you respect, and you should have no trouble.

SELLING HOUSEWARES

The home is still the woman's domain, even the career woman's. And women are much more secure and authoritative when purchasing goods and services for their home than in other buying situations. Consequently, even younger women are likely to want you to use the nice boy approach in these situations.

SELLING WOMEN'S APPAREL

When you sell women's apparel, the rules change again. Here the woman will need you to be a representative male, so that she can judge how other men will see her through your eyes. This means that the sexist-paternalistic role is almost always appropriate.

Here, too, are some fine points and some pitfalls to be avoided. It is important to be credible. If a woman thinks you are flattering her in order to sell her something, she will be extremely insulted and definitely won't buy. It is much more effective—as well as more ethical—to help find the things which really look best on her, and then let her know how well you think she looks.

Women Selling to Men _____

When women sell goods to men, the problems are quite different. Men seldom mind a sexist approach, and usually enjoy a woman who brings a healthy dose of flirtatiousness to her work. Men also tend to feel superior to women in technical matters, as well as anything to do with traditionally male domains, including just about all of business. The woman trying to sell to men in these areas has a dual challenge. She has to convince him that she is competent; at the same time she must flatter his ego so that he feels she looks up to his intelligence.

The winning approach is something of a self-contradiction. Talk about your product in an authoritative and sophisticated manner, but tell him about it in a way that suggests you know that he grasps everything you are telling him.

OLDER WOMEN SELLING TO YOUNGER MEN

If you are an older woman selling to a younger man, the ways in which you talk about your product remain essentially the same, although you are permitted to be a little more authoritative. On the other hand, the role relationship changes from the flirtatious to the maternal. You want to give the man the suggestion that you approve of him, and (providing you get to know him over successive transactions) are proud of him. Perhaps you wish you had a son just like him. Advise him in a way that suggests you take a personal interest in his success.

Summary

The essence of selling through powertalk consists of developing the right image relationship. This means seeing what the needs of your clients' personality (as well as business) are, and projecting an image tailored to fit.

Necessary to all image relationships is an ethical appearance. There are two kinds of ethics: product ethics, where you only represent your product, and client ethics, where you are responsible to the client and his best interests as well. Avoid high-pressure tactics, but there are some closing techniques which are acceptable.

These are basic image relationships:

- The peer approach: highly ethical, emotionally cool, and informative.

- The authoritarian approach: tells the insecure client what to do.

- The conspiratorial approach: shares in the buyer's motives and fantasies, supports his conclusions.

- The victim approach: suggests the customer is getting a bargain or a deal because the salesman is at a disadvantage.

Language can be tailored to what you're selling and orchestrated to build a maximized impact.

There are three approaches that the man who is selling to women has to choose from: sexist-paternalistic, nice boy, and equal. The trick is to let the woman tell you which one she wants.

When women sell to men, a flirtatious, sexist approach is seldom resented. Women have to walk softly when selling men technical items or anything that is specific to the masculine domains. Older women are often successful with a maternalistic approach.

FROM POWERTALK
TO PERSONAL POWER

15

When you began reading *Powertalk!*, you were motivated by the feeling that in some way you didn't command the personal power that you deserve by virtue of your intelligence, accomplishments, and position in life. With my encouragement, you came to hope that by mastering powertalk you would be able to change that. Now you've learned both how to speak powertalk and how to use it in a variety of circumstances and situations. I am sure that you have also begun to practice powertalk as well. If you have, you doubtless realize that you have just begun to scratch the surface of how you can use powertalk, and what it can do for you.

In this brief, final chapter, I want to share a few last thoughts with you on how to continue to master powertalk, and keep growing in personal power.

If you read this book from cover to cover and then put it away without looking at it again, you will have gotten a lot out of it, but you also will have wasted a lot. Although this book was written to interest and inspire you in a first reading, it was also organized so that you can use it as a basic reference. You can return to it, time and time again, as you need to sharpen up your powertalk skills in various circumstances and situations. Keep your copy handy. Skim through it regularly to sustain your motivation to become a master powertalker. Refer to it whenever you have a powertalk task ahead of you and you feel the need to refresh your memory . . . whether it's how to best phrase a sales presentation, how to set limits on your teenager's privileges, or how to handle a confrontation with an intimidating peer. The summaries at the end of each chapter will help you find your way back to the appropriate sections.

Be Codominant at All Times

Your main job, as one who wishes to master powertalk and become more personally powerful, is to strive to relate to others as a codominant at all times (except, of course, when you are trying to dominate). Unshakable codominance is not just a goal; it is a discipline, which (if you follow it actively) will help you develop the skills and strengths that you are seeking.

The way to follow this discipline is to strive to speak positive peertalk at all times, and listen to yourself. Whenever you find yourself slipping into subtalk, stop and ask yourself why you are doing it and what you are trying to accomplish by it. Frequently, you will find that you are being manipulated by a person or a situation you don't know how to handle. Make a mental note of this. Then go back to the book, read the relevant passages, and make a plan for how you can proceed the next time. If you do this regularly, you will find that your ability to function codominantly will constantly develop.

Stay Psychologically Codominant

If you continue to pay attention to the times when you lose codominance and start subtalking, you will notice one thing that is common to all of them: your emotions will have become submissive just before your language did. To enjoy the maximum success in becoming a codominant person, it is not enough to speak the language of power; you must come to feel the emotions of power as well. This is something that will develop gradually as you enjoy success with powertalk, but you can greatly accelerate the process if you strive to remain psychologically codominant, as well as speaking powertalk.

Once again, accomplishing this is a matter of sustained effort and awareness. There are two times during which you can practice developing this awareness. The first is when you actually feel yourself slipping into a submissive frame of mind, and the second is during a tranquil period later in the day. Both are essential, and serve a different function, but they work together.

If you feel yourself slipping into psychological submissiveness during an encounter, you should resist it with your willpower, and force yourself to continue speaking powertalk by applying the skill and knowledge that you have gleaned from this book. You should also make a mental note of what is happening, and observe as much about it as you can.

Later (perhaps the best time is before retiring, but any quiet time will do), review what happened in your mind. Ask yourself what it is about the person, situation, or circumstance that pushed you toward submission. In particular, look for that error or distortion in your own self-image, and ask yourself what a more objective way of seeing yourself might be.

If you are unable to see an error in your self-image, continue looking. You can be assured that one is there. Codominance is the natural state of a healthy person. Whenever a person abandons codominant feelings for submissive ones, they are coming out of a distorted self-image.

Once you are able to see a more objective way of per-

ceiving yourself, replay the entire incident in your mind
from this viewpoint. In other words, imagine how it might
have happened and you might have felt, had you not been
suffering from a negative self-image.

If you practice this reviewing exercise regularly, you
will find that each time you get into a similar situation,
you will have less tendency to submit. You will be able to
powertalk more successfully as a result.

Here is an example to make this entire process clearer.
A woman client of mine was brought up to believe that to
have an opinion that differed from a man's—and to stand
up to him with it—was unfeminine behavior. If she did it,
she was told that no man would find her attractive. Because of this early training, she gave in whenever she was
in a conflict with any man whose opinion of her was of any
concern to her.

In one particular incident, she got into a discussion
with her fiancé about the merits of a nuclear power plant,
which a utility company was planning to build in the
area. She felt strongly about the ecology issue and was
totally opposed to the plant. But her fiancé took a very
money-conscious view, which he expressed forcefully in a
way that seemed almost to mock her concerns. To her
dismay, she heard herself back down and agree with him.

Afterwards, she felt terribly depressed for having
abandoned her convictions. What is more, she felt totally
alienated from her fiancé and even entertained thoughts
that she really had to break up with him. She found herself wanting to find someone who agreed with her and
would respect and listen to her.

When she went through the review exercise, she
realized that she had manipulated herself out of expressing her opinion through her fears of seeming unfeminine. It was her mistaken belief that it was un-
womanly to have strong convictions and stand up to men.
After she became aware of that, she fantasized going
through the entire situation again—only this time fight-

ing for her own beliefs. This exercise made her feel better immediately, and it defused a lot of her anger toward her fiancé. It also made her realize that he wasn't acting insensitive toward her, just speaking his mind in the same way she wanted to do it.

A few days later, a similar situation occurred. This time she was able to resist the impulse to back down, and instead stood her ground and argued the case. To her delight, her fiancé engaged in a real discussion with her, and he seemed more interested in her than before.

This is, of course, just one example. They don't always turn out that well. Sometimes it is a lot harder to see what you are doing and change it; sometimes people will be totally unreceptive to the more codominant you. What is essential is that you dedicate yourself to the process of remaining codominant, working out all of those psychological stumbling blocks which tend to get in the way of using powertalk effectively.

Fight for Dominance When Appropriate ____

Although your primary goal in powertalk is to insist on codominance as a minimum condition in all relationships, codominance alone is not always enough. There will be times in your life when it is not adequate to be codominant; the situation or your convictions will demand that you fight for dominance and control. In fact, there will be times when there is no codominant ground, only a battleground. You can try to avoid these situations, but you can only do that so often and for so long. Beyond a point, it will constitute a kind of cowardice, and eventually will make it impossible for you to remain even codominant.

The way to become a real powertalker and develop your full power potential, is to strive for dominance whenever the situation demands it. Do not back off unless you are totally overwhelmed. This means standing up for your rights in relationships, seeking raises and promotions at work, expressing your opinions in social situations and business meetings, gaining respect from your parents or children. Do all of these things firmly and with dignity, and when necessary don't be afraid to fight.

Getting into the habit of standing up for yourself may be difficult and threatening at first, particularly if it is not natural to you. As you get used to doing it, and get used to succeeding as well, it will get easier and easier.

Fighting for dominance when appropriate, along with always remaining at least codominant, is the choice of the powertalker. They are the two parts of that discipline by which you will master powertalk and develop more personal power. The more you devote yourself to it, the more you will get out of it.

Becoming a Causal Person

Most people are reactive. That is they do not create events; they react to them. Subtalkers are almost totally reactive. They constantly look at what other people do and what they seem to want from them, and then try to please or at least placate. Subtalkers are usually secretly angry as well, because they continually subject their goals to those of others, and get so little of what they really want and need for themselves.

The opposite of a reactive person is a causal one. It is not that causal people are free from the impact of other people's opinions or of external events. No one who lives in the real world can really be that free. It is that causal people respond to things differently. They do not feel that their feelings and reactions are dictated by things outside themselves. Rather, they see these things as opportunities for creativity and problem solving. Furthermore, causal people go through life imagining possibilities, setting goals, and putting events into motion. Causal people tend to create the situations to which reactive ones respond.

The entrepreneurs, the scientists and inventors, the leaders of industry, the innovators and artists—they are all causal people. To become more of a causal person should be your goal as well. In this direction lies the freedom, excitement, creative satisfaction, and financial reward that you want in your life. This is the way to become the center of a world that is largely your own creation where you will find yourself surrounded by people you want to know and who will listen to you and respect you. Powertalk can take you there.

INDEX

absolutes, use of, 24, 38

accents, 60–62, 69

aesthetics, language of, 43

analytical speech, 87–89, 93–94

apologies, 74, 77–78, 83

arguing, the powertalk way, 89–93, 95

authoritative voice, use of the, 23–26, 38

big words, use of, 49

boasting, the powertalk way of, 78–81, 83

body language, 6, 55, 65–69

breath, in powertalk, 59, 69

business world, powertalk in the, 111–12, 151–62
see also employers, powertalking to; salesmanship

business meetings, calling and conducting, 155–62, 205

buzzwords, 46–47

Calero, H.H., 64

causal personality, becoming a, 205

cliches, 51–52

codomination in relationships, 96–97, 101, 103, 106–8, 115, 140–41, 201–2, 204

commands, 72–74, 83

concise language, 75–76, 83, 93, 95

cosubmission in relationships, 106–10, 115

courtesy, 76–77, 83, 101, 108

crime, language of, 46

criticizing others, 129–32

cursing, *see* obscenities

decisiveness as an aspect of powertalk, 5–6, 70–72, 82

de-emphasizers, 26

deference, 108–9, 153, 189

delivery of powertalk, 54–69

diminutives, 50

disclaimers, 30–32, 39

dominant personalities,
    characteristics of, 3–8,
    12, 70
    see also dominating
    others
dominating others, 96–97,
    101, 103, 106, 110–11, 115,
    134, 143–44, 150, 204–5
double-edged words, 49–50,
    136

emotional language, 40, 43,
    89–91, 95
emphatics, 21–22, 37–38
employers and bosses,
    powertalking to, 7,
    152–54, 161, 163–64,
    168–84
enunciation, 62, 69
enthusiasm as an aspect of
    powertalk salesmanship,
    188, 190–91
euphemisms, 53
evidence, use of, 91–93, 95
exercises for powertalking,
    36–37, 201–4
expressive language, 39–41
eye-contact, 62–64, 69

facial expressions, 63–65,
    68–69
factual language, 34–37, 39,
    92–93, 95
family life, powertalk in, 25,
    90–91, 112, 140–50

feelings, language for, 43
"feminine" language, 42–44
fillers, 26, 32–34, 39
formality and powertalk,
    85–86, 94
friends, powertalking to, 90,
    132–35

government agencies,
    powertalking to, 11,
    123–27

*How to Read a Person Like a
    Book,* 64
homemaking, language of,
    43
humility in powertalk,
    78–79, 83
humor, 50, 53, 81, 126–27
hyperbole, 43

industry and labor, language
    of, 46

jargon, 47–48, 51, 196

laughter, role of, in
    powertalk, 65, 69
leadership, qualities of, 3,
    8–9, 152–55, 168, 204–6
logic in powertalk, 84–89, 91,
    93–95

lovers, powertalking to, 90,
    136–40, 150, 203–4

marriage, powertalk in,
    140–45
"masculine" language,
    42–44
money, language of, 45–46
mumbling, 62

Nierenberg, G.L., 64
nonverbal aspects of
    powertalk, 55, 62–65
    see also body language
nurture, language of, 43

objective voice, 35
obscenities, 52–53
office life, effect of powertalk
    in, 10–11, 23
    see also business world,
    powertalk in the
"outside world," powertalk in
    the, 11–12, 116–27

peertalk, negative, 106,
    108–11, 115, 134–35, 150
peertalk, positive, 106–8,
    115, 134, 139–40, 153,
    155, 161, 190, 201
personal life, powertalk in,
    111–12, 128–50
personal qualities, language
    for, 43

pitch, vocal, 58–59, 69
power, fighting for it,
    96–104, 114, 141–42,
    147–48, 150, 202–5
Power Quotient, 8, 13–20,
    112–14, 141
precision with language,
    74–75, 83, 94
problem solving, powertalk
    approaches to, 87–89,
    94–95
professionals, powertalking
    to, 111, 116–22, 126
promises, 78, 83
promotions, 10, 151–52,
    175–84, 204
pronounciation, 62
proverbs, 51–52

qualifying statements, 26,
    28–29, 38

raises, powertalking for,
    163–75, 178–79, 183–84
rhythm, 59–60, 69

salesmanship and powertalk,
    11, 185–99
self-deprecation, 81, 83
service people, powertalking
    to, 11, 122–25, 127
sizing up others, 98–100, 104
slang, 46, 51
smiling, role of, in
    powertalk, 64–65, 69

specialists, speaking to, 47–48, 92–93, 116–22, 126–27, 192–93
specialized language, 44–48
speed of speech, 58–59, 69
sports, language of, 44–45
subjective voice, 35, 39
submissive personalities, characteristics of, 5–8, 12, 70, 107–10, 115–16, 202–3, 105
submissiveness, nonverbal signs of, 62
submissive verbal devices, 21–22, 26–34, 38–39, 138–39
swearing, 52–53

tag statements, 26–29, 38

tone, 6, 94

ultimatums, 164, 174–75, 183

violence, language of, 46
vocabulary of powertalk, 40–53, 84, 87
vocabulary of subtalk, 41, 43–44
vocal projection, 57
voice, role of, in powertalk, 56–59, 68
volume in powertalk speech, 57–58, 69

war, language of, 45